Saint Joseph

NEW AMERICAN CATECHISM

According to the new
National Catechetical Directory
"Sharing the Light of Faith"
and Holy Scripture

No. 2

Middle Grade Edition

Arranged and Explained by

REV LAWRENCE G. LOVASIK, S.V.D.
Divine Word Missionary

W9-CPQ-652

CATHOLIC BOOK PUBLISHING CO.
New York

Dedicated to
SAINT JOSEPH
Patron of the Universal Church

Nihil Obstat: James T. O'Connor, S.T.D.
Censor Librorum

Imprimatur: Joseph T. O'Keefe
Vicar General, Archdiocese of New York

OTHER CATECHISMS BY THE AUTHOR

CATECHISM SKETCHED (Part One: The Creed. Part Two: Sacraments, Commandments, $5.00 each)

CATECHISM IN STORIES (Part One: The Creed. Part Two: Commandments. Part Three: Sacraments. Each Part $2.50).

(Order from: Rev. Lawrence G. Lovasik, S.V.D., 211W 7th Ave. Tarentum, Pa. 15084.

(T-252)

FOREWORD

THE new *National Catechetical Directory* states: "Textbooks must present the authentic and complete message of Christ and His Church, adapted to the capacity of the learners, with balanced emphasis proportionate to the importance of particular truths." (264)

I have tried to follow this important principle of the American Bishops in preparing the four editions of THE NEW AMERICAN CATECHISM. To reach various age levels the Catechism has: The First Communion Catechism (Grades 1-2), the Primary Edition (Grades 3-5), the Middle Grade Edition (Grades 6-8), and the Expanded Edition (High School and Adults).

The text used for the answers was taken from "Basic Teachings for Catholic Religious Education" (National Conference of Catholic Bishops, January 11, 1973), which is now found in a revised form in "Chapter V: Principal Elements of the Christian Message for Catechesis" and "Chapter VI: Catechesis for a Worshiping Community" of *Sharing the Light of Faith* — National Catechetical Directory for Catholics of the United States. References to the revised text are indicated.

In order to make the teaching of these truths more effective, I recommend the use of sketches and stories, which can be found in my two publications listed on the opposite page.

Father Lawrence G. Lovasik, S.V.D.

PRAYER BEFORE INSTRUCTION

Come, Holy Spirit, fill the hearts of your faithful and enkindle in them the fire of your love.

℣. Send forth your Spirit and they shall be created.

℞. And you shall renew the face of the earth.

Let us pray. O God, who have taught the hearts of your faithful people by sending them the light of your Holy Spirit, grant us by the same Spirit to have a right judgment in all things and evermore to rejoice in his holy comfort. Through Christ our Lord. Amen.

PRAYER AFTER INSTRUCTION

Jesus, I come to you. You are the Way that I want to follow in obedience to your commandments, your counsels, and your example. Let me walk after you in the way of obedience, self-denial, and sacrifice, which leads to heaven and to you.

Jesus, you are the Truth. You are "the Light which enlightens every man who comes into this world." I believe in your Gospel. I want to know you that I may love you.

Jesus, you are the Life, through your sanctifying grace which is the life of our souls; through your words which are "the living bread which has come down from heaven"; through your Heart which is the fountain of life for individual souls and for society.

I cling to your word with all my heart. I hunger for the living bread of your Eucharist. I open my heart eagerly to the life-giving streams from Your Sacred Heart. I unite myself inwardly to all its intentions. May this divine Heart reign universally, over the children of the Church and over all humanity. Amen.

CONTENTS

Part Five
THE CHURCH

Part Six
THE SACRAMENTS

Part Seven
SIN

Part Eight
THE LIFE OF GRACE

Part Nine
THE MORAL LIFE

Part Ten
MARY AND THE SAINTS

Part Eleven
DEATH, JUDGMENT, ETERNITY

The Holy Trinity

The Holy Trinity comes to my soul in Baptism

Part One — THE MYSTERY OF ONE GOD

CHAPTER 1 The Holy Trinity

1. **What is the history of salvation?**

   The history of salvation is the story of God's dealing with men.

   The history of salvation tells us how God saved us. It is the plan by which God—the Father, the Son, the Holy Spirit—revealed himself to men, made peace between God and man by his death on the cross, and united with himself those turned away from sin.

2. **How did God deal with men?**

   God (1) revealed himself to man (2) and saved man from sin.

   (1) God made himself known to people. Revelation means that God showed us something of himself. He made himself known to us that he might save us. The Bible tells us about this revelation. The Bible is the written record of God's actions in the world. It is true because it is God's own word, which he made known to the writers of the Bible.

   (2) Sin made us lose God's life. God sent his Son to save us from sin and death, and to give us God's life of grace. Because of his Son God now forgives our sins if we are truly sorry and if we want to be his friends.

9

3. How did God reveal himself in the Old Testament?

God revealed himself in the Old Testament as the one true personal God, and prepared to reveal the Trinity later.

In the Old Testament of the Bible we read about God showing himself to us as the one true personal God. People learned that God was real, that he was faithful to his promises, and that people could be his friends if they put their trust in him.

4. What is the mystery of the Trinity?

The mystery of the Trinity is the one true God in three Persons—the Father, the Son, and the Holy Spirit.

Jesus Christ has revealed to us the secrets of the kingdom of heaven. The greatest of his teachings is the secret of God himself. He has told us of the life of God. Jesus taught us that in the one God there are three Persons, each equal to each other. He told us the names of these three Divine Persons: Father, Son, and Holy Spirit.

God has revealed this mystery to us because he wants us to know him as he is, to know as much about him as we can that we might love him more in return for his boundless love for us.

5. How was the mystery of the Trinity expressed in the New Testament?

The mystery of the Trinity was expressed in the person, words and actions of Jesus Christ.

After speaking through the prophets, God sent his Son. He came among people in the Person of his Son, Jesus Christ. Jesus told us the "Good News" of salvation. This message is found in the New Testament. By his words and actions, and especially in his holy Person, Jesus made known the deepest truths about God. The Blessed Trinity is the deepest of all mysteries.

6. How did Jesus Christ reveal himself?

Jesus Christ revealed himself as the eternal and divine Son of God.

Jesus said that he is the Son, the only-begotten Son of the Father, equal to the Father.

Speaking of himself, Jesus said, "Yes, God so loved the world that he gave his only Son, that whoever believes in him may not die but may have eternal life" (Jn 3, 16).

At the Last Supper he prayed to the Father, "Father, the hour has come! Give glory to your Son that your Son may give glory to you, inasmuch as you have given him authority over all mankind, that he may bestow eternal life on those you gave him. . . . Do you now, Father, give me glory at your side, a glory I had with you before the world began" (Jn 17, 1-2. 5).

Jesus said to his apostles, "All that the Father has belongs to me" (Jn, 16, 15).

Philip once said, "Lord, show us the Father." "Philip," Jesus replied, "after I have been with you all this time, you still do not know me? Whoever has seen me has seen the Father. How can you say, 'Show us the Father'? Do you not believe that I am in the Father and the Father is in me?" (Jn 14, 9-11).

7. Did Jesus reveal the Father?

Jesus more fully revealed the Father.

Jesus constantly spoke of his Father, calling him always by that name. When he drove the money changers from the temple, he said, "Stop turning my Father's house into a market-place!" (Jn 2, 16).

Jesus said to his apostles, "My Father has been glorified in your bearing much fruit and becoming my disciples. As the Father loved me, so I have loved you. Live on in my love" (Jn 15, 8-9).

Jesus taught us to love our heavenly Father because he loves us and wants to help us in all the needs of our body and soul. He wants to bring his children to his heavenly home.

8. **Did Jesus reveal the Holy Spirit?**

Jesus revealed the third Divine Person, the Holy
Spirit, whom the Father and he, as the Risen Lord,
sent to his Church.

Jesus promised to send a third Divine Person, the equal of
himself and the Father.

At the Last Supper he told the apostles, "I will ask the
Father and he will give you another Paraclete—to be with you
always: the Spirit of truth, whom the world cannot accept,
since it neither sees him nor recognizes him; but you can recognize
him because he remains with you and will be within you" (Jn 14,

"The Paraclete whom the Father will send in my name will
instruct you in everything, and remind you of all that I told you"
(Jn 14, 25-26).

"When the Paraclete comes, the Spirit of truth who comes
from the Father—and whom I myself will send from the Father—
he will bear witness on my behalf" (Jn 15, 26).

9. **What did Jesus, the Divine Teacher, teach his disciples?**

The Divine Teacher taught his disciples (1) about the
true God (2) and called them to become sons of God
through the gift of the Spirit.

(1) Since he was God, Jesus could teach us about the true
God. He told his apostles that he is the way to the Father. By
getting to know him they get to know the Father also. They can
see the love of the Father in the actions of Jesus, because Jesus
said that he and his Father are one.

When he sent his apostles to preach the gospel to the whole
world Jesus told them to baptize "in the name of the Father, and
of the Son, and of the Holy Spirit" (Mt 28, 19). Here Jesus expresses the idea of one God (in the name) in three separate and
equal Divine Persons (Father, Son, Holy Spirit).

(2) Jesus called us to become children of God. We become children of God through a new life which he gives us. It is God's own life, given to us by the Holy Spirit. It is called "grace." Because he was the Son of God Jesus was able to give us a share of God's life and make us children of God. He does this through the gift of the Holy Spirit which he gives us.

10. How do we honor the Blessed Trinity?

We honor the Blessed Trinity by trying (1) to remember the presence of God the Father, Son, and Holy Spirit in our soul (2) and to understand, as much as we can through faith, that through baptism we are called to a close union of love with the three Divine Persons.

(1) We show our love for the Blessed Trinity when we remember that the Father, Son, and Holy Spirit are in our soul when we are in the state of grace. Jesus said, "Anyone who loves me will be true to my word, and my Father will love him; we will come to him and make our dwelling place with him" (Jn 14, 23). "I will ask the Father and he will give you another Paraclete— to be with you always" (Jn 14, 16).

We show our love for the Blessed Trinity when we pray to God. We may pray simply to God—to the Blessed Trinity. We may pray to any one of the three Divine Persons. We may pray as the Church does most often—to the Father, through the Son, in union with the Holy Spirit. Jesus said, "Whatever you ask the Father, he will give you in my name" (Jn 16, 23).

(2) God lives in our soul by grace. We first received this grace through baptism. Faith tells us that we are called to a close union of love with the Father, the Son, and the Holy Spirit. We belong to God who is closest to us. God is our Father; Jesus Christ is our Lord and Savior; the Holy Spirit is our teacher and guide.

Teacher reference: Principal Elements, no. 83

A. FILL IN THE BLANKS

(The numeral at the end of each sentence shows which question gives the answer. These answers should be written out on a separate sheet of paper as homework or they can be discussed with the class.)

1. The history of salvation is .... (1)

2. God dwelt with men by (1) .... and by (2) .... (2)

3. God revealed himself in the Old Testament as .... (3)

4. The mystery of the Trinity is .... (4)

5. Jesus Christ revealed himself as .... (6)

6. Jesus revealed the Holy Spirit, whom .... sent to the Church. .... (8)

7. Jesus taught his disciples about .... (9)

8. Jesus called his disciples and us to become .... (9)

9. We honor the Blessed Trinity (1) by .... (10)

10. Through baptism we are called (2) to .... (10)

B. BIBLE READING   Exodus 3, 4-14; 4, 1-17

The Burning Bush

One day Moses, while leading the sheep of his father-in-law near a mountain, was startled by the sight of a bush on fire. He wondered why it did not burn up. He came closer to look at it, and he heard his name called by the voice of God. The voice told Moses to take off his sandals, for the place was holy.

From the bush God spoke to Moses: "I have heard the prayers of the children of Israel. I have seen how they suffer at the hands of the Egyptians. I will deliver them from their masters, and take them to a land flowing with milk and honey. Go to the king of Egypt, and ask him to let the Israelites go to the desert to offer sacrifices."

Then God said to Moses, "Tell them that HE WHO IS has sent you." This is the name by which the Israelites since that time have known God. This name meant the everlasting and faithful God.

Moses and Aaron went to ask the king of Egypt, in the name of the Lord, to let the Israelites go to sacrifice in the desert.

The king answered, "Who is the Lord, that I should hear his voice? I do not know him. I will not let the Israelites go."

Discussion:

1. Why was Moses startled?
2. What did God say to Moses?
3. What name did God give himself?
4. Who helped Moses when he went before the king of Egypt?
5. What did Moses and Aaron ask the king to do?
6. Did the king do what they asked?

C. PRACTICE

1. Think of the Father, Son, and Holy Spirit dwelling in your soul by saying a short prayer like the Glory be to the Father.
2. Make the sign of the cross very carefully.

We offer ourselves to God through Jesus

CHAPTER 2
True Worship of God

11. What must we believe about God?

We must believe that God is all-good, holy, just, and merciful, wise and perfect.

God is all good. He is Love itself. He has given us all the good things we have because he loves us. He created the world to show forth his glory and to share his happiness with the beings he created. He shares his life with them. He loves all men and wills that all men be saved.

God is all-just. He promised to reward those who do good and to punish those who do evil.

God is all-merciful, ready to forgive any sinner who is truly sorry and who wishes to lead a good life.

God is all-wise. He knows all things, past, present, and future, even our secret thoughts, words, and actions. Nothing can be hidden from him.

God is all-perfect. He is all-holy because he is God. He is infinite because there is no limit to his life. He is eternal because he had no beginning and will have no end. He is all-powerful because he can do all things. He is everywhere.

God is the one limitless, almighty, all-knowing spirit. He does not need anything or anyone outside of himself. All things depend on him. Yet God cares for all things which he has created. He calls all men to become his adopted children.

16

12. **How has God shown his love for us?**

God has shown his love for us (1) by making firm promises to men and drawing them to himself by solemn agreements; (2) he freed and saved us; (3) he loves each of us with the love of a father and always cares for us.

(1) After our first parents, Adam and Eve, sinned, God made a promise to save all men. He kept his promise. He chose Abraham's descendants to be his own special people. With the help of Moses the Jewish people made a contract with God, called the "Covenant." God made known his will in the Ten Commandments. Though Israel broke the Covenant, God did not forsake his people. At last he came among his people in the person of his Son. A New Covenant was made in his blood by his death on the cross.

(2) Through Jesus Christ God shows his love for us. He made known to us his loving plan of salvation. Now he even shares his life with us through Jesus. Through the suffering, death, and resurrection of Jesus we have received grace and God's life. Through him we have hope of eternal life with God in heaven.

(3) God truly loves us and takes care of us as a loving Father. He has made us his children through baptism and has prepared his heavenly kingdom to be our eternal home.

13. **What should the thought of God's goodness do for us?**

The thought of God's goodness (1) should make us find joy in the God who gives us eternal hope (2) and should prompt us to worship him.

(1) We belong to God. He loves us and asks that we love him so that we may be with him forever in heaven. God's love for us should make us trust him and find our joy in him.

(2) We owe God loving service and worship. We show our loving service by obedience to his will. We worship him by our love and adoration.

14. How do we worship God?

We worship God (1) especially in the sacred liturgy, offering ourselves to him through our Lord Jesus Christ, (2) by doing his will in all our actions; (3) by using well the talents he has given us.

(1) We worship God especially when we adore him in the Holy Sacrifice of the Mass. We offer ourselves to him with the offering of Jesus. We worship God also when we pray to him.

(2) We worship God when we do his will by keeping his commandments as obedient children.

(3) We are in this world to know God, to love and serve him, and to use our talents in his service.

15. What should we hope for from the goodness of God?

From the goodness of God we hope to receive the grace we need to live a life of love for God and neighbor for his glory.

We trust that God will help us to live a life of love for him and our fellow men. We live a life of love when we devote ourselves to our Creator. God will give us his help to love him as he wants us to love him. Our life can be very happy if only we open our hearts to him and try to use the graces he offers us each day to honor him and to help the people around us.

16. Why do many people today pay little attention to God?

Many people today pay little attention to God because modern life is taken up with man rather than with God.

God continues to be good to us, and yet there are very many people in the world who hardly ever think of him; many even break his commandments. They are too interested in their own pleasures and in the things the world offers them.

We must accept God's word with deep faith and trust in his love for us, for he is faithful to his promises. But many people are not ready to believe in God.

17. **Does every man have some desire for God?**

No matter how hidden, some desire for God is in the heart of every man.

God has made us for himself and we cannot find true happiness unless we look for it in him. Even when we do not want to think so, there is a secret desire in our hearts for God. Since God has helped us to know him more than many other people do, he expects us to love him more and serve him better. Our life will be blessed if we do so, and we can look forward to being with God forever in heaven. *Teacher reference: Principal Elements, no. 84*

A. FILL IN THE BLANKS

1. We must believe that God is all-good, ... (11)

2. God has shown his love for us (1) by ....
   (2) .... (3) ....
   .... (12)

3. The thought of God's goodness (1) should ....
   and should (2) .... (13)

4. We worship God (1) especially in the sacred liturgy by ....
   .... (2) by doing his will in ....
   (3) by using well .... (14)

5. From the goodness of God we hope .... to
   live a life of .... (15)

6. Many people today pay little attention to God because ....
   .... (16)

7. No matter how hidden, ... is in the heart of
   every man. (17)

B. BIBLE READING

Genesis 22, 1-18

The Sacrifice of Abraham

When Abraham was a hundred years old, Sarah, gave him a son. They called him "Isaac," meaning "Laughter," for Sarah said, "God has made me laugh, and everyone who hears of it shall laugh with me."

Abraham and Sarah loved Isaac with all their hearts because he had been sent as God had promised, to make them happy in their old age. But God wanted to test Abraham, to see whether he loved his son more than he loved God. One night God said to Abraham, "Take Isaac and go to a mountain that I shall show you. There offer me your son as a sacrifice."

Abraham became very sad. As he had always obeyed God, he was ready to obey him now. He cut wood for the sacrifice. With two servants and his son, he set out to find the place that God would show him.

After three days they came to a mountain called Mount Moriah. Abraham said to his servants, "Stay here while Isaac and I go up the mountain to offer a sacrifice."

Abraham placed the wood upon the shoulders of Isaac, while he himself carried the fire and a knife. As they were going up the mountain, Isaac asked, "Father, we have the fire and wood, but where is the victim for the sacrifice?"

His father answered, "God will give us a victim for the sacrifice."

When they came to the place for the sacrifice, they made an altar and put the wood upon it. Then Abraham tied Isaac and laid him upon the wood.

Just as Abraham was about to strike his son with the knife, an angel touched his hand and said, "Abraham, do not kill your son. God knows now that you truly love him, for you are ready to sacrifice Isaac at his command."

These words made Abraham very happy. He saw a sheep caught in the bushes. He took the sheep and offered it to God as a sacrifice, instead of his son.

Then the angel told Abraham that God would bless him for this offering he had made, that he would have very many descendants, and that from his family the Savior of the world would one day be born.

Discussion:

1. Why did God want to test Abraham?
2. How did Abraham worship God?
3. Why did the angel keep Abraham from killing his son?
4. Why is Isaac carrying the wood up the mountain a picture of Jesus our Savior?
5. Why did the heavenly Father let his own Son die on the cross?
6. How did God reward Abraham for his love and obedience?

C. PRACTICE

1. Remember that it is your duty to worship God, especially on Sunday, the Lord's day. You worship God by offering the Holy Sacrifice of the Mass in his honor. Do this with all the love of your heart.
2. Be obedient to God no matter how hard it may be to obey him. Be obedient especially to your parents who have a right to tell you what you must do.

God gave me life through my Parents

Part Two — CREATION

CHAPTER **3** The beginning of the History of Salvation

18 What is creation?

Creation means that God made the whole universe out of nothing.

Creation is the way God gave life and the world to man. We owe all that we have to God. The Bible does not try to explain creation. God's people knew that he was Lord of life and the universe.

19. What did the action of God in the Old Testament show and prove?

The action of God in the Old Testament (1) showed his power (2) and proved that he is always with his people.

(1) In the Old Testament God's people learned the truth of God's almighty power in the creation.

(2) His power in creation reminded the people that God remains always with his people to protect and help them. His wonderful deeds of power and victory show that he kept his promises and that he loved his people.

20. **What is the beginning of the mystery of salvation?**

The creation of angels and of the world is the beginning of the mystery of salvation.

Long before God created man, he made the angels. They were spirits, meaning that they had no body. They had a brilliant mind to understand God's goodness and beauty; they had a free will to love and praise him. Some of the angels sinned and became evil spirits.

21. **What is the first gift of God leading to Christ?**

The creation of man is the first gift of God leading to Christ.

Man has a mind to know his Creator and a will to love him. To reach eternal happiness with God man must freely accept God's love and devote himself to his service. But Jesus is the one whom God sent to lead people to God. It is only through him that we can be saved. That is why we can say that the creation of man is the first gift of God leading to Christ.

22. **Where is the all-powerful action of God for our salvation especially seen?**

The all-powerful action of God for our salvation is especially seen in Christ's resurrection from the dead.

Though he was made by God in a state of holiness, man turned against God of his own free will, being led to do so by the evil spirit. God sent his Son to free man from the slavery of sin and to make him holy again. He did this through the sufferings and death of Jesus and through his glorious resurrection. In this way God showed his all-powerful action for our salvation.

23. **How should we look upon creation?**

We should look upon creation as God's continuing action as he works out the salvation of men.

When we think of the creation of the angels, the world, and man, we should see how God's all-powerful action saved all men. His great love for man led him to do so. The whole work of salvation receives its meaning from Jesus Christ, the incarnate Word. That work, beginning with the creation, showed itself in Christ's coming, his life on earth, his death and resurrection, and will show itself at his second glorious coming, which will complete the work of God.

24. How was God present in human history?

God was present in the history of Israel; he was powerfully at work in the life, death, and resurrection of his Incarnate Son.

When we hear about the creation, we not only should think of God's act of making the world, but we should turn our mind to all that he did to save the people in this world. His deeds of salvation can be seen in the history of man and of the world, especially in the history of Israel. They lead to the most important events in our Lord's life, his death and resurrection.

25. How is God present among us today?

God is lovingly present in human history using his limitless power to help us. He will finish his saving work only at the end of the world.

The life, death, and resurrection of Jesus is the most important event of all time through which God shows himself and his love for man. He also shows himself in other events which are found in the Bible and in the life of the Church. God will continue to be present among us, showing his power and his love.

Teacher reference: Principal Elements, no. 86

A. FILL IN THE BLANKS

1. Creation means that .... (18)

2. The all-powerful action of God in the Old Testament (1) showed .... (2) and proved that .... (19)

3. The creation .... is the beginning of the mystery of salvation. (20)

4. The .... is the first gift of God leading to Christ. (21)

5. The all-powerful action of God is especially seen in .... (22)

6. We should look upon creation as .... as he works out .... (23)

7. God was present in ....; he was powerfully at work in .... of his Incarnate Son. (24)

8. God is lovingly present in human history using .... He will finish his saving work only at .... (25)

B. BIBLE READING   Genesis 1
God Created All Things

God had no beginning and he will have no end. He is eternal.

God made the angels. They are spirits like the soul of man. Lucifer was one of the most glorious and most beautiful of the angels. His name means "Bearer of Light." He became very proud and even wanted to be as great as God himself. He cried out against God, "I will not serve!" With him were other angels who also refused to obey God.

But the Archangel Michael cried out, "Who is like God?" Other good angels joined him in a great battle against Lucifer and his bad angels, and drove the bad ones into a place of eternal punishment. We call Lucifer "Satan," and his bad angels "devils."

To have a beautiful place for man to live, God made the universe.

God Created All Things

On the first day God made earth out of nothing. Then God said, "Let light be made," and at once light appeared. God separated light from darkness and called them day and night.

On the second day God made the blue sky and called it heaven.

On the third day God said, "Let the waters under heaven be gathered together into one place, and let the dry land appear. Let this dry land bring forth grass and trees and plants of every kind."

On the fourth day God made the sun, the moon, and the stars.

On the fifth day God made the fishes and other creatures that were to live in the water. He also made birds and other creatures that were to fly in the sky.

On the sixth day God made all the animals that were to live on the ground. Then God said, "I shall make man in my image. I shall make man to rule over all the things that I have created." God formed man out of the dust of the earth. Then he breathed into him a soul that will never die.

On the seventh day God rested from his work. He blessed that day and made it holy.

Discussion:

1. Who are the angels?
2. How did the angels sin against God?
3. What did the Archangel Michael and the other good angels do?
4. What did God make on the first day? On the second day? On the third day? On the fourth day? On the fifth day? On the sixth day? What happened on the seventh day?

C. PRACTICE

1. Everything in the world was created to give glory to God. We, the greatest of all his earthly creatures, must praise God and love him with all our hearts. We should thank God for the beautiful things we see around us. Our greatest thanksgiving is Holy Mass.

2. Often during the day say a little prayer to thank God for the good things you receive from him. Thank God in the beautiful prayer: Glory be to the Father and to the Son and to the Holy Spirit, as it was in the beginning, is now, and ever shall be, world without end. Amen.

Jesus spoke about the things God made

4 Knowledge of God and the Witness of Christian Love

26. **Can man come to know God through created things?**

(1) Sacred Scripture says that man can come to know God through the things God has made. (2) The Church teaches that from thinking about created things man can come to know God as the beginning and end of all that is.

(1) The God who loves us makes himself known to us in various ways. He teaches us through the things he has made. The Bible tells us that man can come to know him through the things he made.

(2) The Church also teaches that created things around us help us to see that the one who made them is God and that he can do all things. If we really love God, we will try to learn as much as we can about him, even from the things he made.

27. How can we help unbelievers to find God?

We can help unbelievers to find God by the witness of (1) a life of firm faith in God, (2) a life of personal love of Christ, (3) a life of goodness and love.

(1) We can help people to turn to God if we give them a good example of our own deep faith in God.

(2) If people see our love for Christ in our good deeds, they will be moved to love him also.

(3) God has willed that all men should make up one family and treat one another in a spirit of brotherhood, for all men are called to the same goal—God himself. By our love for one another for the love of God and by other good works we can help those who do not believe in God to find him.

28. What is our duty toward the world?

Faith in God and union with Christ also mean that we must help men to solve their problems as much as we can.

We show our love for God also by loving our neighbor—the people around us. Love for our neighbor makes us do all we can to help those who need our help and make the world better.

Teacher reference: Principal Elements, no. 86

A. FILL IN THE BLANKS

1. Sacred Scripture says .... through the things God has made. (26)

2. The Church teaches that man can come to know God as the beginning and end of all that is from .... (26)

3. We can help unbelievers to find God by the witness: (1) of a life of .... (2) of a life of .... (3) of a life of .... (27)

4. Faith in God union with Christ also means that we must help men to .... (28)

B. BIBLE READING   1 Samuel 17, 32-51

David and Goliath

Once the Philistines built their camp on one mountain; the Israelites pitched theirs on the opposite mountain.

Out of the Philistines' camp came a ten-foot giant named Goliath. He was covered with bronze armor. He called out to the Israelites, "Choose a man from among you. Let him come down to fight me. If he kills me, we will be your servants. If I kill him, then you shall become our servants."

Saul and the Israelites were very much afraid. Many days passed. Still no Israelite dared to fight Goliath. One day David arrived at the Israelite camp to see his three brothers who were in Saul's army. He heard the giant shouting, "I defy you, Israelites! Give me a man, so that we may fight together."

David asked, "Who is this man who defies the army of God? I will fight him!"

"You cannot fight Goliath," said Saul; "you are only a boy and he has fought many battles."

"I have killed both a lion and a bear that took a lamb of my father's flock. God, who protected me from those wild animals, will protect me against this Philistine giant," answered David.

So David took his shepherd's staff and his sling in his hand, and picked out five smooth stones from the brook and went to meet Goliath.

The giant came forward to meet his enemy. A shield-bearer marched in front of him. When he saw coming toward him only a boy, the giant was angry and roared, "Am I a dog that you come to me with a staff? Come, and I will feed you to the birds!"

And David said, "You come to me with a sword, a spear, and a shield. I come in the name of God, who will deliver you into my hands."

Then the boy took a stone and put it in his sling and shot it. The stone struck Goliath in the forehead and he fell to the ground. David took the giant's sword and cut off his head.

Then David was given a place of honor among the fighting men of Israel. And all the people loved David.

Discussion:

1. Why was not David afraid to fight the giant?
2. What did David say to the giant before he killed him?
3. How did David kill the giant?
4. How did David give a good example to the godless Philistines?

C. PRACTICE

1. When you see the fields and lakes, flowers and animals, the stars in the sky, think of God who created these creatures to let you know more about himself. Make an act of love when you see God's goodness.
2. Try to help others to turn to God by coming to Mass faithfully and by being kind to people.
3. Pray that people who do not know God may come to know him.

THE BIBLE . . .

They devoted themselves to the apostles' instruction and the communal life, to the breaking of bread and the prayers. A reverent fear overtook them all, for many wonders and signs were performed by the apostles. Those who believed shared all things in common; they would sell their property and goods, dividing everything on the basis of each one's need. They went to the temple area together every day, while in their homes they broke bread. With exultant and sincere hearts they took their meals in common, praising God and winning the approval of all the people. Day by day the Lord added to their number those who were being saved.   (Acts 2, 42-47)

Since the creation of the world, invisible realities, God's eternal power and divinity, have become visible, recognized through the things he has made. Therefore these men are inexcusable.   (Rom 1, 20)

The heavens declare the glory of God, and the firmament proclaims his handiwork.   (Ps 19, 1)

Petitions to Jesus

O good Jesus: Word of the Eternal Father, convert me.
Son of Mary, take me as her child.
My Master, teach me.
Prince of Peace, give me peace.
My Refuge, receive me.
My Shepherd, feed my soul.
Model of patience, comfort me.

Meek and humble of Heart, help me to become like you.
My Redeemer, save me.
My God and my All, possess me.
The true Way, direct me.
Eternal Truth, instruct me.

Life of the saints, make me live in you.
My Support, strengthen me.
My Justice, justify me.
My Mediator with your Father, reconcile me.
Physician of my soul, heal me.
My Judge, pardon me.
My King, rule me.
My Sanctification, sanctify me.
Abyss of goodness, pardon me.

Living Bread from Heaven, nourish me.
Father of the prodigal, receive me.
Joy of my soul, be my only happiness.
My Helper, assist me.
My Protector, defend me.
My Hope, sustain me.
Object of my love, refresh me.
My Divine Victim, atone for me.
My Last End, let me possess You.
My Glory, glorify me. Amen.

Jesus, the Way, the Truth, and the Life

CHAPTER

5   Jesus Christ, Son of God, the Firstborn of All Creation, and Savior

29. What is the greatest of God's works?

The greatest of God's works is the taking on of human flesh by his Son, Jesus Christ, and this is called the incarnation.

The greatest of God's works is the incarnation of his Son, Jesus Christ. The incarnation means that the Second Person of the Blessed Trinity, the Son of God, the Divine Word, became man and came to live among us.

30. Why did the Son come on earth?

The Son came on earth (1) to bring the world his own divine life (2) and to save it from sin, (3) and in this way to make the world new again from within.

(1) Born of the Virgin Mary, the Son of God has truly been made one of us, like us in all things except sin. The human race lost God's life of grace through sin, the sin of our first parents. Because of his love for us Jesus brought grace back to us by his life, death, and resurrection. He showed us what it means to be a child of God.

(2) Jesus offered his life as the highest gift to his Father by dying on the cross for us. In this way he redeemed the world. The passion and death of our Lord teaches us the great evil of sin. It

35

was sin which caused him to suffer so much and to die. But he took away our sins and made us free to serve God and to reach heaven.

(3) Jesus showed us how we must belong to God. His whole life was devoted to doing the work and will of his Father. To receive God's life we must accept Jesus and his way of life. We do this through baptism. Through the Catholic Church and its truth and sacraments we are able to keep this life in our soul. With this grace we can be united with God in this world and forever in heaven. Through his grace Jesus is for us a source of life and salvation from sin. In this way he renews the world from within.

31. Why is Jesus Christ called the Firstborn of all creation?

Jesus Christ is the Firstborn of all creation because he is before all—all things have been created in him, through him, and for him.

"He is the image of the invisible God, the first-born of all creatures" (Col 1, 15). This perfect image of God is the first-born in the order of creation because Christ is the most excellent of all creatures as well as their Creator.

32. How was Jesus Christ made known to us as God's Son in power?

Through his resurrection Jesus was made known to us as God's Son in power, for he was obedient unto death and exalted as Lord of all.

God chose his Son to be the one to suffer and to die for our sins. Because of his obedience he was raised up as Lord of all. By conquering death through his own power in his resurrection, Jesus has shown himself Master of life and death. Therefore he is true God and true man, our Savior.

33. **What has Jesus Christ done for us through his resurrection?**

Being the Firstborn of the dead, (1) Jesus Christ gives eternal life to all, (2) and in him we are made new men.

(1) When Christ passed from death to life he brought about our passing from the death of sin to life in him.

(2) We receive the new life of grace in baptism because in Christ we are created new men. We are now God's children. St. Peter says, "Praised be the God and Father of our Lord Jesus Christ, he who in his great mercy gave us new birth; a birth unto hope which draws its life from the resurrection of Jesus Christ from the dead; a birth to an imperishable inheritance . . . which is kept in heaven for you" (1 Pt 1, 3-4).

34. **Why is Jesus Christ our Savior?**

Jesus Christ is our Savior because through him all creatures will be saved from the slavery of sin.

St. Paul speaks of sin as a slavery. Jesus is our Savior because he saved us from sin.

35. **Is there any other Savior?**

There is no salvation in anyone but Jesus Christ, nor has there ever been.

All stand in need of Christ, their Savior, for by his own power no one is freed from the slavery of sin. Scripture says, "There is no salvation in anyone else" (Acts 4, 13).

Teacher reference: Principal Elements, no. 87

The Birth of Jesus.

A. FILL IN THE BLANKS

1. The greatest of God's works is ....

   and this is called the .... (29)

2. The Son came on earth (1) to .... (2)

   and to .... (3) and in this way to .... (30)

3. Jesus Christ is the Firstborn of all creation because ....

   all things have been created .... him, ... him, and

   .... him. (31)

4. Through his .... Jesus was made known to us as

   ...., for he was .... and .... (32)

5. Being the Firstborn of the dead Jesus Christ gives ....,

   (2) and in him .... (33)

6. Jesus Christ is our Savior because through him ....

   .... of sin. (34)

7. There is no salvation in anyone but .... nor

   has there ever been. (35)

B. BIBLE READING
Luke 2, 1-7

The Birth of Jesus

Soon after the birth of John the Baptist, Joseph had a dream. He saw an angel from the Lord standing beside him. The angel said, "Joseph, son of David, do not be afraid to take Mary as your wife, for that which is begotten in her is of the Holy Spirit. And she shall bring forth a Son, and you shall call his name Jesus; for he shall save his people from their sins."

Soon after Joseph and Mary were married in Nazareth, a command went forth from the Emperor, Caesar Augustus, through all the lands of the Roman Empire. All the people were to go to the cities and towns from which their families had come, and there to have their names written down upon a list. Since both Joseph and Mary had come from the family of King David, they went together from Nazareth to Bethlehem. It was a long journey.

When Joseph and Mary came to Bethlehem, they found the city full of people who, like themselves, had come to have their names written upon the list. The inn was full, and there was no room for them. The best they could do was to go to a stable, where the cattle were kept. In this stable of Bethlehem Jesus, the Savior of the world, was born.

Mary wrapped her Child in swaddling clothes and laid him in a manger, where the cows and oxen were fed. Then she and Joseph adored the Divine Infant. This was the very first Christmas.

Discussion:

1. What did the angel tell Joseph in his dream?
2. Why did Joseph and Mary travel to Bethlehem?
3. Why did Joseph and Mary have to go to a stable for the night?
4. What did Mary do after Jesus was born?
5. What feast is celebrated in memory of the birth of our Lord?

C. PRACTICE

1. The prayer which reminds us of the scene of the Annunciation, the moment when God became man, is the "Hail Mary." This prayer contains the words of Scripture itself, the greeting of the angel to Mary and the greeting of her cousin Elizabeth to the Mother of God. We should say this prayer often every day.

2. When we receive Holy Communion we receive the same Jesus who was made man for us—his body and blood, soul and divinity. We should try to love Jesus more through our frequent Holy Communions.

Jesus speaks:

"Whoever has seen me has seen the Father. How can you say, 'Show us the Father'? Do you not believe that I am in the Father and the Father is in me?"   (Jn 14, 9, 10)

"You became a believer because you saw me. Blest are they who have not seen and have believed."   (Jn 20, 29)

Jesus said to Pilate "I am a King"

CHAPTER 6   Jesus Christ, the Center of All God's Saving Works

36. What is God's plan for us?

The carrying out of God's plan for us is the story of man's salvation—to form his people into "the whole Christ."

Jesus Christ gave himself for us in his passion that he might redeem us from sin and make us a people pleasing to God. He then sent the Holy Spirit, the spirit of adoption, to make us children of God. In this way he made in himself a new people, filled with the grace of God. United with Jesus, the new people of God are "the whole Christ." He offers them to his Father and gives him glory. This is the Father's plan for the salvation of all men.

37. Why is Jesus Christ the center of all God's saving works?

Christ is the center of all God's saving works because the Christian can fulfill his task of making creation give glory to God through the power of Jesus the Savior.

Jesus Christ became man so that as perfect man he might save all men and sum up all things in himself. He summed up in himself the mysteries of our salvation by his death and resurrection; he received all power in heaven and on earth; he founded his Church as a means of our salvation. So in Christ, our Redeemer, we are joined to all men.

41

Since Christ is the center of all God's works of salvation, through him we can make all creation give glory to God. All this was made possible through his love and power. God is the full meaning of life and Jesus is the way to God. Jesus asks us to believe in him and put our hope in him for the future, and to love him with all our heart. Jesus said, "The Father loves the Son and has given everything over to him. Whoever believes in the Son has life eternal" (Jn 3, 35-36).

Teacher reference: Principal Elements, no. 88

A. FILL IN THE BLANKS

1. The carrying out of God's plan for us is .... (36)
2. The story of man's salvation is to .... (36)
3. Christ is the center of all God's saving works because ....
   .... through the power of .... (37)

B. BIBLE READING   Matthew 17, 1-9
The Transfiguration

Jesus and his apostles were passing by a mountain. It was our Lord's custom to leave the apostles, especially in the evening, and go to a quiet place to pray. Jesus left the apostles at the foot of the mountain and took with him only Peter, James, and John. They went up the mountain to pray.

While Jesus was praying, a great change came over him. His face began to shine as brightly as the sun, and his clothes became whiter than snow. The three apostles saw their Lord with all this glory beaming from him.

And they saw two men talking with Jesus. These were Moses and Elijah, who had come down from heaven to meet Jesus. They represented the Law and the Prophets that had announced the coming of Jesus. Now they spoke with him of the death that he was to die in Jerusalem.

Scarcely knowing what he was saying, Peter spoke, "Master, it is good for us to be here! If you wish, let us set up three tents here, one for you, one for Moses, and one for Elijah!"

While Peter was speaking, a bright cloud came over them all. The three apostles felt a great fear as they found themselves in the cloud. Out of the cloud the apostles heard a voice saying, "This is my beloved Son, in whom I am well pleased; hear him."

As the apostles heard this voice, they fell down upon their faces on the ground in great fear. And Jesus came and touched them, saying, "Arise, and do not be afraid."

Then they looked up, the bright cloud had passed away, and Jesus was standing there alone. They walked together down the mountain, and Jesus said to them, "Do not tell to any man what you have seen, until the Son of Man is risen from the dead."

Discussion:

1. Whom did Jesus take with him when he went up the mountain to pray?
2. What happened to Jesus while he was praying?
3. Why did Moses and Elijah appear?
4. What did Peter say to Jesus?
5. What were the words of the heavenly Father?
6. What did Jesus say to his three apostles when they were frightened by the voice?
7. What did Jesus say to them when they were walking down the mountain?

C. PRACTICE

1. The Church worships God in the highest way in the Holy Sacrifice of the Mass. At the end of the Eucharistic prayer the Church says: "Through him (that is, through Christ), with him, in him, in the unity of the Holy Spirit, all glory and honor is yours, almighty Father, forever and ever. Amen." At each Mass offer yourself to God through Jesus so that God may be praised.

2. Since Jesus is the center of all God's works of salvation, we should turn to him with great confidence in his love and power to help us to lead a good Christian life and to save our soul.

JESUS SPEAKS:

The Father loves the Son and has given everything over to him. Whoever believes in the Son has life eternal." (Jn 3, 35-36)

THE BIBLE . . .

It is he who gave apostles, prophets, evangelists, pastors and teachers in roles of service for the faithful to build up the body of Christ, till we become one in faith and in the knowledge of God's Son, and form that perfect man who is Christ come to full stature. (Eph 4, 11-13)

When, finally, all has been subjected to the Son, he will then subject himself to the One who made all things subject to him, so that God may be all in all. (1 Cor 15, 28)

Jesus told the high priest that He is the Son of God

CHAPTER 7 **Jesus Christ, True God and True Man**

38. **Why is Jesus true God?**

Jesus is true God because he is God's only-begotten Son, and in him there is all fullness of divinity.

Jesus Christ is true God, the Son of the heavenly Father, the Divine Word of God made man. But he is only one Person; and that Person is the Second Person of the Blessed Trinity. St. John wrote: "In the beginning was the Word; the Word was in God's presence, and the Word was God" (Jn 1, 1).

Jesus said he was God. He said to the Jews, "These very works which I perform testify on my behalf that the Father has sent me" (Jn 5, 36). "I tell what I have seen in the Father's presence" (Jn 8, 38).

At the trial of Jesus the high priest said to him, "I order you to tell us under oath before the living God whether you are the Messiah, the Son of God." Jesus answered, "It is you who say it. But I tell you this: Soon you will see the Son of Man seated at the right hand of the Power and coming on the clouds of heaven" (Mt 26, 63-64).

The night before Jesus died he prayed, "Father, the hour has come! Give glory to your Son that your Son may give glory to you, inasmuch as you have given him authority over all mankind, that he may bestow eternal life on those you gave him" (Jn 17, 1-2).

39. How does the creed express our faith in the divinity of Christ?

The Nicene Creed says of Jesus Christ: "God from God, light from light, true God from true God, begotten not made, of one substance with the Father."

The chief teaching of the Catholic Church about Jesus Christ is that he is God made man. It is Jesus Christ the God-Man whom we see and hear in the gospels and receive in the Eucharist. It is to him with the Father and the Holy Spirit that we pray: Glory be to the Father, and to the Son, and to the Holy Spirit.

40. Why is Jesus Christ true man?

Jesus Christ is true man because he, the Son of God, was "manifested in the flesh" (1 Tm 3, 16). (1) As man, he thought with a human mind, acted with a human heart. (2) He joined himself with every human being except in sin.

(1) The Son of God became a real man, having real flesh, a human body and soul. He is a man just as we are. He felt the joys and sorrows, pleasures and pains that we feel as human beings. As man Jesus had a human mind, a human will, to know and to love as we do. This means that he was born into this world, and lived a real human life.

Mary was the mother of Jesus. He was conceived by the Holy Spirit within her. Joseph was Mary's husband and acted as foster father to Jesus during childhood. Jesus died just as the rest of us must.

(2) Jesus joined himself with us in all things except in sin. He is the all-holy God. The human nature he assumed never knew sin.

41. How did Jesus show his concern for men?

Jesus lived among men, was close to them, reached out to all—the virtuous and sinner, the poor and the rich, especially the suffering.

Jesus was kind to all people and spent his life helping them in their needs. He traveled all over Israel, teaching the people about his Father and working miracles. His whole teaching was about loving God with our whole heart and our neighbor for his sake. He loved especially the poor, the sick, and the troubled.

Jesus loved sinners and forgave their sins. He offered his life to save all mankind.

42. What do we see in Christ's concern for men?

In Christ's concern for men we see God's love for man.

We cannot see God, but when God sent his Son to live among us and to save us by his death on the cross, we can see how much God really loves us.

Teacher reference: Principal Elements, no. 89

A. FILL IN THE BLANKS

1. Jesus is true God because .... and in him there is .... (38)

2. Jesus is true God from ...., begotten ...., of one substance .... (39)

3. Jesus Christ is true man because he, the Son ...., was .... (40)

4. As man, Jesus thought with a human ...., acted with a human ...., loved with a human .... (40)

5. Jesus joined himself with every human being except in .... (40)

6. Jesus was close to men, the virtuous and ....,
   the poor and ...., especially .... (41)

7. In Christ's concern for men we see .... (42)

B. BIBLE READING   John 11, 1-43

Lazarus Raised from the Dead

Martha and Mary sent word to Jesus that Lazarus, their brother, was sick. Two days later Lazarus died.

Now Martha heard that Jesus was coming, and she went to meet him.

Jesus said to her, "Your brother shall be alive again."

"I know that he will be alive again in the resurrection, at the last day," said Martha.

Jesus said, "I am the resurrection and the life; he who believes in me, even if he die, shall live; and whoever lives and believes in me shall never die. Do you believe this?"

"Yes, Master," said Martha, "I believe that you are the Christ, the Son of God."

Now Mary came and bowed in sorrow at the feet of Jesus. And seeing her tears and the grief of friends who stood there, Jesus wept.

And he came to the tomb, which was a cave with a stone at the entrance.

"Take away the stone," said Jesus.

"But, Master!" cried Martha, "Lazarus has been dead and in the tomb for the past four days!"

Jesus said, "Have I not said to you, 'Believe, and you will see the glory of God'?"

So they moved away the stone. And Jesus turned to God in prayer. "Father, I thank you that you have heard me. I know that you always hear me; yet I say this because of the people standing here, so that they may believe that you sent me."

Then he called with a loud voice, "Lazarus, come forth!"

And the man who had been dead came out, though his hands and feet were still wrapped with linen. Jesus said to those who were near, "Unbind him, and set him free."

Jesus raises Lazarus from the dead.

Many of the Jews believed in him and said, "See how he loved him!"

Discussion:

1. What did Jesus say to Martha?
2. What did Martha say to Jesus when he asked whether she believed in him?
3. How did Jesus pray to his Father?
4. How did Jesus raise Lazarus from the dead?
5. Why did this miracle prove that Jesus is true God?
6. How did this miracle show that Jesus was true man?

C. PRACTICE

1. We worship Jesus Christ even in his human nature because that human nature belongs to the Second Divine Person, the eternal Son of God. At Mass we offer Jesus, who died for us on the cross as a sacrifice to the heavenly Father. At Holy Communion Jesus comes to us as God and man to be the food of our soul.

2. We can worship Christ in his human nature also through devotion to the Sacred Heart of Jesus. The heart of Jesus is here taken as a symbol of his manhood and of the infinite love of Christ and the mercy he has for sinners. Devotion to the Sacred Heart of Jesus in the Blessed Sacrament is one of the best means of growing in our love for him.

JESUS SPEAKS:

"These very works which I perform testify on my behalf that the Father has sent me" (Jn 5, 36). "I tell what I have seen in the Father's presence. . . . Were God your father you would love me, for I came forth from God, and am here. . . . I know him well, and I keep his word. . . . I solemnly declare it: before Abraham came to be, I am." (Jn 8, 38. 42. 55. 58)

"Father, the hour has come! Give glory to your Son that your Son may give glory to you, inasmuch as you have given him authority over all mankind, that he may bestow eternal life on those you gave him. . . . Do you now, Father, give me glory at your side, a glory I had with you before the world began." (Jn 17, 1-5)

Jesus is our Redeemer

Jesus Christ, Savior and Redeemer of the World

43. Why is Jesus Christ our Savior and Redeemer

Jesus Christ is our Savior and Redeemer because as God made man (1) he preached the gospel of the kingdom of God (2) and gave himself up to death out of love for his Father and for us.

God sent his Son to free men from the power of Satan and make peace between God and men. To do this Jesus had to become man, to preach his truth about the kingdom of his Father. He said to the people, "The reign of God is at hand! Reform your lives and believes in the gospel!" (Mk 1, 15). Jesus continued preaching even though the religious leaders of the Jewish people were trying to harm him. They finally arranged to have him put to death by the Romans because he claimed to be the Son of God. Jesus is truly our Savior.

(2) Jesus is also our Redeemer because he paid our debt for sin and bought heaven back for us. He offered his life for the love of us and for the glory of his Father. He did his Father's will to honor him and to make people happy forever in God's kingdom. The Father now gives his own divine life of grace to people who turn to him in faith.

44. How did Christ redeem mankind?

By his death and resurrection Christ redeemed mankind from slavery to sin and to the devil.

In obedience to his Father's will Jesus gave himself for us in his passion and arose from the dead that he might redeem us from sin and make us a people pleasing to the Father. He is the Messiah, God's own Son. He often said that what he was doing was done that the Scriptures might be fulfilled, because he saw his Father's will in them. We were slaves of the devil because of original sin and because of our personal sins. But Jesus made us free with the freedom of the children of God, for by his resurrection he destroyed death and gave us the life of grace.

45. How does the risen Lord now help us?

Risen truly, the Lord (1) gives us the divine life of grace (2) and pours out his Holy Spirit upon us.

(1) By dying Jesus destroyed our death and by rising he gave back our life. He now shares with us his divine life of grace, especially through the sacraments.

(2) Jesus gives us his Holy Spirit to make us holy and pleasing to God. We must live the life of God as Jesus did. The Father gives his own life to people who turn to him in faith. The Father, Son, and Holy Spirit come and share their love with those who give themselves to Jesus. In this way Jesus makes us a new People of God.

Teacher reference: Principal Elements, no. 90

A. FILL IN THE BLANKS

1. Jesus is our Savior and Redeemer because as ....
   (1) he preached .... (2) and .... (43)
2. Jesus gave himself up to death out of love for .... (43)
3. By his .... Christ redeemed mankind from .... (44)
4. Risen truly, the Lord (1) gives us .... (2) and
   pours out .... (45)

B. BIBLE READING   Matthew 27, 32-54

Jesus Dies on the Cross

When Calvary was reached, the soldiers stripped the clothes of Jesus from his bruised body. Into his hands and feet they hammered a heavy nail, while the blood flowed freely. Then they lifted him up in mid-air. Pilate had this sign put on the cross: "Jesus of Nazareth, the King of the Jews."

Jesus prayed on the cross, "Father, forgive them, for they do not know what they are doing." Two robbers were hung on crosses, one at his right side and the other at his left. One of them said to Jesus, "Lord, remember me when you come into your kingdom."

And Jesus answered him, "Amen I say to you, this day you shall be with me in paradise."

Standing by the cross of Jesus was his mother, and beside her was John, the disciple whom he loved best. Other women besides his mother were there—his mother's relatives and Mary Magdalene. Jesus wished to give his mother into the care of John, now that he was leaving her, and he said to her, as he looked from her to John, "Woman, behold your son."

In the middle of the afternoon when Jesus had endured three hours of terrible pain on the cross, he cried out, "My God, my God, why have you forsaken me?"

After this he spoke again, saying, "I thirst." Someone dipped a sponge into a cup of vinegar and put it upon a reed and gave him a drink of it.

Then Jesus spoke his last words upon the cross, "It is finished! Father, into your hands I give my spirit!"

Discussion:

1. What sign did Pilate have placed on the cross?
2. What prayer did Jesus say for those who crucified him?
3. How did Jesus pray to his Father from the cross?
4. What did Jesus say to his mother before he died?
5. Why did Jesus die on the cross?

C. PRACTICE

1. The best way to honor Jesus Christ, our Savior and Redeemer, is to offer the Holy Sacrifice of the Mass in union with him. The Mass is the unbloody memorial and renewal of the sacrifice of the cross. At Mass we remember the love of Jesus who gave his life to save us, and we receive his sacrificed and risen body in Holy Communion.

2. All Catholic churches have a series of fourteen pictures showing the various scenes in the passion and death of Jesus, called "The Stations of the Cross." This devotion is one of the most highly blessed devotions in the Church, and one which will give us a deeper understanding of the love and mercy of God as well as a greater sorrow for our sins.

The Father and the Son sent us the Holy Spirit

Part Four — THE HOLY SPIRIT

CHAPTER
9

The Holy Spirit in the Church and in the Life of the Christian

46. Who is the Holy Spirit?

The Holy Spirit is God, and Third Person of the Holy Trinity.

The Holy Spirit is the Third Person of the Blessed Trinity, really God, the same as the Father and the Son are really God. He is the love of the Father and the Son.

47. What is the work of the Holy Spirit in the world?

The Holy Spirit carries out Christ's work when persons answer God's invitation to love him and one another.

The Holy Spirit was already at work in the world before Jesus rose from the dead and ascended into heaven. But to finish the work of the salvation of all men, Jesus sent the Holy Spirit from the Father. The Spirit now carries out his work of salvation in the souls of men and spreads the Church throughout the world among people who are willing to answer God's invitation to love him and one another.

48. What did Christ say about the Holy Spirit?

Christ promised that this Spirit of Truth (1) would come (2) and would remain within us.

Jesus promised to send the Holy Spirit when he said to his apostles, "I will ask the Father and he will give you another Paraclete—to be with you always: the Spirit of truth, whom the world cannot accept, since it neither sees him nor recognizes him; but you can recognize him because he remains with you and will be within you" (Jn 14, 16-17).

49. When did the Holy Spirit come into the world?

The Holy Spirit came at Pentecost, never to depart.

Fifty days after Easter, on Pentecost Sunday, the Holy Spirit came to the early Church and changed the apostles from weak fearful men to brave men of faith that Christ needed to spread his gospel to the nations.

50. Where is the Holy Spirit present in a special way?

The Holy Spirit is present in a special way in the Church, the community of those who believe in Christ as Lord.

The Holy Spirit is present in the Catholic Church to help it to continue the work of Christ in the world. By his presence people are moved by his grace to unite themselves with God and men in sincere love and to fulfill their duties to God and man. He makes the Church pleasing to God because of the divine life of grace which he gives. By the power of the gospel he makes the Church grow. He renews with his gifts, and leads it to perfect union with Jesus.

51. What does the Holy Spirit do for the Church?

The Holy Spirit gives his divine life of grace to the Church.

Before ascending into heaven, Jesus gave his apostles a command to teach all nations and to baptize them. He promised to be with them. "Teach them to carry out everything I have commanded you. And know that I am with you always, until the end of the world!" (Mt 28, 20).

Jesus is with his Church also through the gift of the Holy Spirit. He promised this the night before he died. "It is much better for you that I go. If I fail to go, the Paraclete will never come to you, whereas if I go, I will send him to you" (Jn 16, 7).

Through the Holy Spirit the Church is able to carry on the work of salvation given to it by Christ. The crucified and risen Jesus leads men to the Father by sending the Holy Spirit upon the People of God. The Holy Spirit came to remain with the Church forever. The Church was publicly made known to the people. The gospel began to spread among the nations. Today the Holy Spirit is still the soul of the apostolate of the Church.

The Holy Spirit guides the Pope, bishops, and priests of the Church in their work of teaching Christ's doctrine, guiding souls and giving God's grace to the people through the sacraments. He directs all the work of Christ in the Church—the care of the sick, the teaching of children, the guidance of youth, the comforting of the sorrowful, the support of the needy.

The Holy Spirit guides the People of God in knowing the truth. He prays in them and makes them remember that they are adopted sons of God. He brings the Church together in love and worship.

52. How should we honor the Holy Spirit?

We should honor the Holy Spirit (1) by loving him as our God (2) and by letting him guide us in life.

(1) We should love and honor the indwelling Spirit as our God as we honor the Father and the Son. St. Paul reminds us to do so. "Are you not aware that you are the temple of God, and that the Spirit of God dwells in you?" (1 Cor 3, 16).

(2) Since the Holy Spirit is always with us if we are in the state of grace, we should often ask him for the light and strength we need to live a holy life and to save our soul.

Teacher reference: Principal Elements, no. 92

A. FILL IN THE BLANKS

1. The Holy Spirit is ...., the .... Person of the Holy Trinity. (46)
2. The Holy Spirit carries out .... when persons answer God's invitation to .... (47)
3. Christ promised that (1) the Spirit of Truth .... (2) and would .... (48)
4. The Holy Spirit came at .... (49)
5. The Holy Spirit is present in a special way in ...., the community of those who .... (50)
6. The Holy Spirit gives .... to the Church. (51)
7. We should honor the Holy Spirit (1) by...................... (2) and by .... (52)

B. BIBLE READING   Acts of the Apostles 2, 1-13
The Descent of the Holy Spirit

After our Lord's ascension into heaven, his apostles and disciples gathered in an upper room with Mary his mother, and the holy women, numbering about one hundred and twenty persons. They spent their time in prayer.

On the tenth day a sound like a mighty wind filled the whole house, and tongues of fire came down upon the head of each one of them. The apostles were filled with the Holy Spirit and began to speak in many strange tongues.

Before the descent of the Holy Spirit, the apostles were afraid. After they had received the Holy Spirit, they were filled with courage and feared nothing. Peter, who had denied his Master three times, came forth with the other apostles, and stood before the crowd. "Men of Israel," he said, "hear these words: Jesus of Nazareth whom you have crucified and put to death by the hands of wicked men, God has raised up. We are all witnesses. And now that he has been taken up into heaven and is at the right hand of God, he has poured forth his Holy Spirit, which you see and hear, even as he promised."

The Coming of the Holy Spirit

About three thousand persons were converted by this first sermon. They were baptized and united with the rest of the disciples. And they continued faithfully in the teaching of the apostles and in the communion of the breaking of the bread and in prayer.

After the feast of Pentecost, the apostles went out into the world and preached Christ crucified. They performed many miracles and converted many people.

Discussion:

1. Who were present in the upper room in prayer?
2. How did the Holy Spirit come upon the people in the upper room?
3. What did Peter say to the crowd on Pentecost?
4. How many people were converted on that day?
5. What did the apostles do after Pentecost?

C. PRACTICE

1. Since the Holy Spirit is the soul of the Church, the Mystical Body of Christ, he joins the members of the Church to one another and to Christ, their Head. Through his grace he is the cause of every good action in all parts of the Body. We should pray to him for the growth of the Church in members and in holiness.
2. Since the Holy Spirit is personally present and active in all the members of the Church, we should love him as we love the Father and the Son in the Holy Trinity. He is our friend and the loving guest of our soul through his grace. We should turn to to him for help that we may live a good Christian life by loving God and our neighbor.

JESUS SPEAKS:

"I will ask the Father and he will give you another Paraclete —to be with you always: the Spirit of truth, whom the world cannot accept, since it neither sees him nor recognizes him; but you can recognize him because he remains with you and will be within you."   (Jn 14, 16. 17)

"The Paraclete, the Holy Spirit whom the Father will send in my name, will instruct you in everything, and remind you of all that I told you."   (Jn 1 , 25. 26)

Jesus is our
Good Shepherd
through the
Holy Priesthood

Part Five — THE CHURCH

<table>
<tr><td>CHAPTER
10</td><td># The Church,
People of God</td></tr>
</table>

53. **When did the Church begin?**
The Church, founded by Christ, began in his death and resurrection.

Through his death and resurrection, Jesus has earned for us the privilege of belonging to God's holy family. To enter that family we need sanctifying grace, a sharing in the life of Christ. We first get grace when we are baptized. By the power of the resurrection, we are inserted into the Mystical Body of Christ. We are no longer under the dominion of sin; with him we are heirs of heaven; we, like him, shall rise from the dead.

The Church officially began when the Holy Spirit entered into the followers of Jesus on the day of Pentecost. The apostles announced to everybody the good news of what Jesus had done and invited their hearers to believe in him and live by his Spirit.

54. What is the Church?

The Church is the new People of God, prepared for in the Old Testament, and given life, growth, and direction by Christ in the Holy Spirit. It is the work of God's saving love in Christ.

Through Israel, the first People of God, God kept his promise to send the world a Savior who would gather all men into God's family. Jesus, God's own Son, born of Mary, was a descendant of David. He brought peace to his people and freed their souls from sin. He is our Savior. Jesus sent his Spirit and life upon his followers as he promised. To proclaim the Good News of salvation to all men everywhere in all time Jesus formed into one body his followers, the community of believers, the new People of God. He called this body his Church.

55. What are the gifts of God in the Catholic Church?

The gifts of God in the Catholic Church are (1) the truths of faith, (2) the sacraments, (3) and the ministries inherited from the apostles.

(1) To carry on Christ's teaching the apostles were given the power and duty to teach his doctrine to the world. They were appointed by him to be our shepherds or spiritual rulers so that through them and their successors he would lead us to the kingdom of heaven. Jesus said, "He who hears you, hears me. He who rejects you, rejects me. And he who rejects me, rejects him who sent me" (Lk 10, 16).

(2) Christ taught the apostles that his grace was to be given to men through them. Through them he would forgive sin, give his Body and Blood to the world, and teach people in his name. Through the apostles and their successors, to whom these powers were entrusted, the Church administers the sacraments for the salvation of God's People.

(3) With the powers given them by Christ the apostles were to be his witnesses in the world. He said to them before ascending

into heaven, "You will receive power when the Holy Spirit comes down on you; then you are to be my witnesses in Jerusalem, throughout Judea and Samaria, yes, even to the ends of the earth" (Acts 1, 8). Jesus continued, through his apostles and their successors, to be king, priest, and teacher to his people.

56. What does the Church do for mankind through these gifts?

Through these gifts of God, (1) the Church is able to act and grow as a community in Christ, (2) serving mankind and giving men his saving word and activity.

(1) Through God's truth and sacraments and the ministry of the priesthood the Church is able to grow. Peter was Christ's chief ambassador on earth. The whole Church was entrusted to his care. The apostles share their responsibility with others, called bishops.

(2) Today Christ continues, through his bishops, aided by priests, to be a community in Christ and to serve mankind by giving men Christ's saving truth and his divine life through grace and the sacraments.

57. Why is the Church missionary?

The Church is missionary because every member of the Church shares the command from Christ to carry the Good News of Christ's teaching to all mankind by word and example.

The Church gives Christian witness as a community of believers and brotherly love by the preaching of the gospel and by its service to others. Jesus said to his apostles, "Full authority has been given to me both in heaven and on earth; go, therefore, and make disciples of all the nations. Baptize them in the name 'of the Father, and of the Son, and of the Holy Spirit.' Teach

them to carry out everything I have commanded you. And know
that I am with you always, until the end of the world!" (Mt 28,
18-20).

58. Why is the Church a society with leaders?

In God's plan, the Church is a society with leaders,
that is, with a hierarchy. It is a people guided by its
bishops, who are in union with the Pope.

Through ordination of bishops and priests the powers of
Jesus Christ have been handed down in the Catholic Church for
nineteen hundred years. Bishops and priests are those in Christ's
Mystical Body who have the authority to teach for Christ, to shepherd his flock and to dispense his graces to the world. Christ lives
and works through his bishops and priests in his Church.

59. Who is the Pope?

The Pope, the Bishop of Rome, (1) is the Vicar of
Christ, who has succeeded to the office of Peter in his
care and guidance of the whole flock of Christ, (2)
and is the head of the college of bishops.

(1) The Pope, the Bishop of Rome, is the successor of St.
Peter, being supreme shepherd of the Church of Christ, having all
the rights, powers and duties of Peter.

(2) Jesus solemnly told Peter he was to be supreme shepherd,
the head of the Church. "I for my part declare to you, you are
'Rock,' and on this rock I will build my church, and the jaws of
death shall not prevail against it. I will entrust to you the keys
of the kingdom of heaven. Whatever you declare bound on earth
shall be bound in heaven; whatever you declare loosed on earth
shall be loosed in heaven" (Mt 16, 18-19).

(3) While the Pope is the successor of St. Peter, the Catholic
bishops are the successors of the other apostles. Christ made the
apostles as a stable group or college. They were jointly responsi-

ble for spreading the gospel of Christ in the whole world. Jesus said to Peter, "I have prayed for you that your faith may never fail. You in turn must strengthen your brothers" (Lk 22, 32). When the Church teaches solemnly in the name of God, the teaching is infallible, that is, it cannot be mistaken in matters of faith or morals.

60. **What is the role of the Pope and bishops in the Church?**

The role of the Pope and the bishops is to teach, to make holy, and to govern the Church.

Christ conferred on the apostles and their successors the duty of teaching, sanctifying, and ruling in his name and power. When a third time Jesus asked Peter, "Simon, son of John, do you love me?" Peter was hurt because he had asked a third time, "Do you love me?" So he said to him: "Lord, you know everything. You know well that I love you." Jesus said to him, "Feed my sheep" (Jn 21, 17).

61. **What do the faithful owe the Pope and bishops?**

The faithful, the community of faith, owe the Pope and bishops respect and obedience.

We serve God and his Church by obeying the Fourth Commandment of God in honoring, loving, respecting, and obeying the Pope as successor of St. Peter, our bishop who is our shepherd and our priests ordained for the loving service of the faithful.

62. **What is the work of the Holy Spirit in the Church?**

(1) The Holy Spirit preserves the Church as the body of Christ and his bride so that it may be faithful to him in holiness till the end of the world. (2) He also helps the Church always to purify and renew itself and its members.

(1) The Holy Spirit brings about a union between Christ and his members. St. Paul describes this union as the Body of Christ. Christ himself is head of that Body, while those who belong to him are its members. They are united closely with the head and with each other by a strong interior bond, which is the Holy Spirit.

The Church is also called the Bride of Christ. St. Paul says that Jesus loved his bride, the Church. He made her beautiful and gave his life for her.

(2) With the help of grace of the Holy Spirit the Church is constantly purified and renewed spiritually. Without these helps of actual grace it is impossible to do anything toward our own salvation or the salvation of others. These graces help us to live well as God's children and followers of Jesus Christ.

Teacher reference: Principal Elements, no. 93

A. FILL IN THE BLANKS

1. The Church, founded by .... began in .... (53)

2. The Church is ...., prepared for in ....,
   and given life, growth, and direction by .... in the ....
   It is the work of .... (54)

3. The gifts of God in the Catholic Church are (1) the ....,
   (2) the ...., and the .... inherited
   from .... (55)

4. Through these gifts of God, the Church (1) is able to ....,
   ...., (2) .... and giving men .... (56)

5. The Church is missionary because each member of the Church
   shares the command from Christ to .... by
   word and example (57)

6. In God's plan, the Church is ...., that is, with............
   .... It is a people guided by ...., who
   are in union with .... (58)

7. The Pope, the Bishop of Rome, (1) is ...., who has
   succeeded to the office of .... in his care and guidance
   of the whole flock of Christ, (2) and is .... (59)

8. The role of the Pope and the bishops is to ...., to
   ...., and to .... the Church. (60)

9. The faithful, the community of ...., owe the Pope and bishops .... (61)

10. The work of the Holy Spirit is: (1) to .... so that it may be faithful to him in .... till the end of the world, (2) and to .... the Church always to............ and .... itself and its members. (62)

B. BIBLE READING   Matthew 16, 13-20

Peter, the Head of the Church

One day, Jesus and his apostles arrived at a place called Caesarea Philippi. There Jesus asked his apostles this question, "Who do men say the Son of Man is?" This was the name by which Jesus often spoke of himself.

They answered him, "Some say John the Baptizer; and others, Elijah; and others, Jeremiah, or one of the prophets."

Then he said to them, "But who do you say that I am?"

Simon Peter answered and said, "You are the Messiah, the Son of the living God!"

Jesus said to Peter, "Blest are you, Simon son of John! No mere man has revealed this to you, but my heavenly Father. I for

my part declare to you, you are 'Rock,' and on this rock I will build my church, and the jaws of death shall not prevail against it. I will entrust to you the keys of the kingdom of heaven. Whatever you declare bound on earth shall be bound in heaven; whatever you declare loosed on earth shall be loosed in heaven."

By these words Jesus promised to make Peter the head of his Church. Keys are a symbol of power. Jesus meant that Peter was to have power to rule his Church.

Discussion:

1. Who did people think Jesus was?
2. Who did Peter say Jesus was?
3. Why did Jesus say Peter was blest?
4. What did Jesus say to Peter about his Church?
5. What did these words of Jesus to Peter mean?
6. Who is the successor of Peter today?

C. PRACTICE

1. Catholic laymen have a part in the mission of the Church. By the very fact of their membership in the Mystical Body of Christ they have a share in the apostolate of the Church. Part of the Church's task is to form the conscience of the individual Christian in order that he might bring the principles of Christ into education, marriage, recreation, business, politics, etc. The Catholic layman must be a witness to Christ in the world and by prayer and good example share in the missionary apostolate of the Church.

2. In making Peter the supreme pastor of his flock Christ gave him the gift of infallibility in matters of faith and morals. Since Peter is the foundation and rock upon which the Church of Christ rests and has the keys by which he can allow men to enter or be excluded from the kingdom of heaven, it follows that he must be infallible. When the Pope speaks he is giving the ordinary teaching of the Church. This teaching is found in papal decrees and encyclicals. We must not only show outward obedience, but also give our assent, at least out of obedience to the teaching Church.

We share together
the Life of Christ

11   The Church as Community

63. Why is the Church a community?

The Church is a community because it shares together the life of Christ; it is a people assembled by God.

The Church is the worldwide community of those whom God has called to give witness to his Son Jesus and to the new life he has brought to men. As members of this community, we are joined to Christ through baptism; we share his divine life through grace which reaches us especially through the sacraments.

64. Are all persons equal in the Church?

All persons in the Church are united and equal as the one People of God.

All members in the Church are united and equal, but they have different responsibilities. Just as God made Moses the leader of his people in the Old Testament, so Christ gave to his apostles and their successors the right to teach and to command in his name. These powers are given for the service and welfare of the whole People of God. Living in the world, the laity are called to work for the sanctification of the world by carrying out their tasks according to the spirit of the gospel.

65. Who has a vocation to holiness in the Church?

In the Church every individual has a call from God, a vocation to holiness.

With Christ we have already died to sin and risen to new-ness of life. He pours into our souls that very life of divine sonship that filled him in his own resurrection. This he does through the sacraments of the Church he founded. In the Church Jesus wishes to continue his own life in us for the glory of the Father. This Christ-life within us is the holiness to which God has called every person in the Church. This is a life of love and obedience to the Father.

66. Why does each member of the Church deserve respect?

Each member of the Church deserves respect, since all join in the one cause of Christ.

Dedication to Christ means obeying the commandments, fulfilling the duties of our state of life, accepting the suffering God permits in our life, striving to do all for the love of God, and working to spread the reign of Christ. Everyone in the Church who in this way joins in the one cause of Christ deserves our deepest respect. Besides, through baptism we united in the Body of Christ of which he is the head.

67. Who directs the work in the cause of Christ in the Church?

The Pope and the bishops direct the work in the cause of Christ in the Church, in every rite, diocese, parish, and mission.

The Pope is a visible sign of Jesus and the symbol of unity for the Church. Together with the bishops, and as their head, he is the universal teacher and governor of the Church. The bishops are visible signs of Jesus in each locality and the symbol of unity for the Church there. Each diocesan bishop is the principal teacher and governor of the Church in that locality. Throughout the world, all the bishops, together with the Pope, are the official witnesses to the faith of the whole Church and are responsible for its life, aided by the priests.

68. Is Christ present in each parish, diocese, and mission?

In each diocese, parish, and mission Christ is present, and by his power the one, holy, Catholic and Apostolic Church is gathered together.

Throughout the grace of the sacraments of baptism and the Eucharist Christ is present in us. The Christ-life within us means that we open our minds to him by faith so that we have the same outlook that he had. We open our hearts to him that he may live in us his own life of love and dedication to the Father. By this power the Catholic Church is gathered together even in the smallest parish.   *Teacher reference: Principal Elements, no. 94*

A. FILL IN THE BLANKS

1. The Church is a community because ....; it is .... assembled by God (63)
2. All people in the Church are united and equal as .... (64)
3. In the Church every individual has a call from God, a vocation to .... (65)
4. Each member of the Church deserves respect, since .... (66)
5. The work of the cause of Christ in the Church is directed by .... (67)
6. Christ is present in each ...., and ...., and by his power the one, holy, Catholic and Apostolic Church is .... (68)

B. BIBLE READING   Matthew 5, 1-16

The Sermon on the Mount

Seeing the great crowd of people following him, Jesus went up to the side of a mountain and sat down where all the people could see and hear him. These are some of the things which Jesus said that day:

The Sermon on the Mount

"Blest are the poor in spirit: the reign of God is theirs. Blest are the sorrowing: they shall be consoled. Blest are the lowly: they shall inherit the land.

"Blest are they who hunger and thirst for holiness: they shall have their fill." Jesus meant that those people are blessed whose longing to be good is just as real as hunger and thirst. God gives good hearts to those who long for them.

Jesus said, "Blest are they who show mercy: mercy shall be theirs." If we are kind to those who are weak and sinful and suffering, God will remember it, and will be kind to us when we are weak and sinful.

"Blest are the single-hearted: for they shall see God. Blest are the peacemakers: they shall be called sons of God. Blest are those persecuted for holiness' sake: the reign of God is theirs."

You have the blessing of Jesus when you try to do right, although your companions may make fun of you and try to stop you. When men sneer at you and say bad things about you because you are trying to do the right thing, do not be discouraged. Be glad, for you will have a great reward in heaven.

Jesus also said, "You are the salt of the earth. But what if salt goes flat? How can you restore its flavor? Then it is good for nothing but to be thrown out and trampled underfoot. You are the light of the world. A city set on a hill cannot be hidden. Men do not light a lamp and then put it under a bushel basket. They set it on a stand where it gives light to all in the house. In the same way, your light must shine before men so that they may see goodness in your acts and give praise to your heavenly Father."

When we love Jesus we are like the salt of the earth. As salt preserves things from rotting, we can keep the world from evil by our good example. We are the salt of the earth in the measure that we are holy.

As Jesus is the light of the world by his holy doctrine and example, so too we may be the light of the world by the brightness of our good example. By the light of our holy life we can scatter the darkness of the spirit of the world.

Discussion:

1. What did Jesus say about those who are poor in spirit? About those who are sorrowing? About the lowly?
2. What did Jesus say about those who hunger and thirst for holiness? About those who show mercy?
3. What did Jesus say about the single-hearted? About the peacemakers? About those persecuted for holiness' sake?
4. Why did Jesus say we should be the salt of the earth?
5. Why did Jesus say we should be the light of the world?
6. How can we see from Christ's words that everyone in the Church is called to holiness?

C. PRACTICE

1. Through Jesus Christ we have been made members of the family of God. We are joined to Christ and one another in a union which is far closer than any union on earth. Our Lord himself compared it to the marvelous union of the Blessed Trinity. Because we belong to the family of God we are a community, we are never alone. We are one with Christ and one with one another in the union of the Mystical Body of Christ here on earth. So close is this union that whatever we do or fail to do to one another we do or fail to do to Christ himself. The things which separate us from one another—wealth, social position, color of skin, difference in nationality—are all small compared to the bond which unites us as members of Christ and one another. We must ever keep in mind the important fact that whatever we do to any man we do to Christ. We should make an effort to see Christ in our neighbor.

2. The center of the parish and the source of its life is Christ. He is truly present in the Eucharist. He is also present in the people who have the divine life of grace, but not in the sacramental way as in the Holy Eucharist. Christ is present, too, among the community of Christians who meet with him in their midst. Through their meeting with one another in a spirit of brotherly love the people of the parish are a witness of Christ's presence among them. They are the sign by which the world can know them as members of Christ's kingdom.

JESUS SPEAKS:

"Treat others the way you would have them treat you: this sums up the law and the prophets."   (Mt 7, 12)

"It was not you who chose me, it was I who chose you to go forth and bear fruit. Your fruit must endure, so that all you ask the Father in my name he will give you."   (Jn 15, 16)

Jesus wants one fold and one shepherd

12 The Quest for Unity

69. Why is Christian unity in faith and love God's will?

Christian unity in faith and love is God's Will because Christ willed that all who believe in him be one, so that the world might know that he was sent by the Father.

There is but one Church. Jesus brought the same good news to all men and called all to the same new life. His Church is the union of those who follow his call. The Roman Catholic Church is the worldwide community of the followers of Jesus that is united around the Pope. The night before he died Jesus prayed for Christian unity. "I pray also for those who will believe in me through their word, that all may be one as you, Father, are in me, and I in you; I pray that they may be one in us, that the world may believe that you sent me" (Jn 17, 20-21).

70. How should Catholics promote Christian unity?

Catholics should (1) be deeply concerned over the sad divisions of Christians, (2) take the first steps in meeting with non-Catholics, (3) and try to make the Church more faithful to Christ and to what it received from the apostles.

(1) Christians are not one because historical differences and bitterness have driven the followers of Jesus apart. Men's understanding of Jesus and the meaning of his life and teaching also differs.

(2) Prayer and work for Christian unity are important to Catholic life. Catholics should take the first steps in meeting with non-Catholics.

(3) Catholics should help to fulfill the Church's mission in our time. They should carry out the gospel of Christ in their own life and dedicate themselves to extend his message to others.

71. What do we believe concerning the Catholic Church?

We believe that the Catholic Church is the ordinary means of salvation, and should desire to share her fullness with all men.

We believe that Jesus Christ entrusted his work of redemption to his Church. He said to his first disciples, "As the Father sent me, so I send you" (Jn 20, 21). Not to the individual, but to the Church was the promise made by Christ: "I will ask the Father and he will give you another Paraclete—to be with you always" (Jn 14, 16).

We believe that only through the Church can we know with certainty what God wills us to believe and to do in order to reach salvation. Only through the Church can we find the security and certainty about the meaning of our human lives.

We believe the Catholic Church has the ordinary means of salvation. She has God's truth, and the sacraments, which are the channels of God's grace.

72. Why should Catholics show respect for all men of good will?

A unity of all men under God should be a concern of Catholics because God has given to every man dignity, freedom, and eternal importance.

Man, because he has a spiritual soul, has dominion over the other earthly creatures and is a more perfect image of God than anything else on this earth. Man is made for God. He has a special dignity and value as a human being. He is free and he will live forever. This makes him deserving of our respect.

As Christ sent his apostles to teach and to be witnesses to him in the world, so too, he wants us to share in this mission. The duty of proclaiming the gospel and making its power felt in the lives of men belongs not only to bishops and priests, but also to the laity in the Church. Every Catholic man and woman is called by God to be an apostle, a messenger of Christ to the world. Therefore the unity of all men under God should be our concern that our Lord's prayer for unity may be fulfilled.

Teacher reference: Principal Elements, no. 95

A. FILL IN THE BLANKS

1. Christian unity in faith and love is God's will because .... so that the world might know that .... **(69)**
2. Catholics should promote Christian unity (1) by being ...., (2) by taking the first steps in ...., (3) and by trying to make the Church more faithful to .... and to .... **(70)**
3. We believe that the Catholic Church is ...., and should desire to .... **(71)**
4. A unity of all men under God should be a concern of Catholics because .... **(72)**

B. BIBLE READING   John 10, 11-18
The Good Shepherd

When Jesus was talking to the crowds, he said, "I am the good shepherd; the good shepherd lays down his life for the sheep. The hired hand—who is no shepherd or owner of the sheep—catches sight of the wolf coming and runs away, leaving the sheep to be snatched and scattered by the wolf. That is because he works for pay; he has no concern for the sheep."

Jesus continued his talk. "I am the good shepherd. I know my sheep and my sheep know me in the same way that the **Father** knows me and I know the **Father**; for these sheep I will give my life.

Jesus — the Good Shepherd.

"I have other sheep that do not belong to this fold. I must lead them, too, and they shall hear my voice. There shall be one flock then, one shepherd.

"The Father loves me for this: that I lay down my life to take it up again. No one takes it from me; I lay it down freely. I have power to lay it down, and I have power to take it up again. This command I received from my Father."

Discussion:

1. What does the good shepherd do for his sheep?
2. What does the hired hand do when the wolf comes?
3. How does Jesus know his sheep?
4. What does Jesus do for his sheep?
5. What does Jesus say about the other sheep that do not belong to his fold?
6. How does the story of the good shepherd show the need for Christian unity?

C. PRACTICE

1. Jesus Christ took to himself one Mystical Body. That Body is the Catholic Church. In the course of history, disputes, misunderstandings, the pride and greed of men, weaknesses and abuses within the Church itself have resulted in harm to the Body of Christ. Millions have been separated from the unity of the Body. Many good people today are deprived, through no fault of their own, of the life-giving sacraments and of sharing in Christ's sacrifice. Christ wants all of them to be re-united to his Mystical Body, the Catholic Church. Even though these people are not aware that the Church is the one true Church of Christ, it is through the Church that they receive their divine life and their salvation. Hence the Church urges Catholics to promote Christian unity by understanding and concern for the separated Christians, by taking the first steps in meeting with them, by being a good example for them and by praying for the unity which Jesus desired as he prayed to his heavenly Father.

2. Much of the tension between Catholics, Protestants, and Jews is the result of misunderstanding, which in turn is the result of lack of contact between those of various faiths. While Catholics may not closely participate in worship with Protestants and Jews, they may and should do so on other levels, such as in civic projects, social works, discussions, and ecumenical services. Such contact will bring about a better understanding.

JESUS SPEAKS:

    "I do not pray for them alone. I pray also for those who will believe in me through their word, that all may be one as you, Father, are in me, and I in you; I pray that they may be one in us, that the world may believe that you sent me."   (Jn 17, 20-21)

Go into the whole, World, Baptize... and Teach

CHAPTER **13** **The Church as Institution for Salvation**

73. **Why is the Church an institution for salvation?**

The Church is an institution for salvation because it is a community of the People of God with Christ as leader and head, who has given it the mission of bringing the message of salvation to all men.

Through Jesus Christ we have been made members of the family of God, the People of God. We are one with Christ and one with one another in the union of the Mystical Body of Christ here on earth. So close is this union that whatever we do or fail to do to one another we do or fail to do to Christ himself.

The Church speaks the good news of God's doings in the world. It does this through its teaching and preaching, through its life and worship, through its Bible and the writings of its prophets. The mission of the Church is to bring the message of salvation to all men. The Church must live the life of Jesus in his Spirit, and show his love by its life of brotherhood and service to others.

74. **What is the role of the Church in the world?**

The Church is not of this world, but it speaks and listens to the world, and tries to be seen by the world as faithful to the Gospel and as journeying toward heaven.

To his Church Christ gave the command to spread the message of salvation to all parts of the earth. God revealed his plan to save mankind and to give each man a share in his divine life through Jesus Christ his Son. Therefore the Church both speaks and listens to the world, without accepting the spirit of the world.

The Church ministers to man's spiritual needs by providing a community of faith, where people can find help and guidance in seeking God. The sacraments are special actions in the Church through which the life of God is given to his people.

The Church also ministers to the bodily needs of people by helping those in need, by overcoming the causes of suffering and by building up a better life for man. But the Church always has heaven in view, and continues to be a light to lead people to eternal life with God.   *Teacher reference:*
Principal Elements, no. 96

A. FILL IN THE BLANKS

1. The Church is an institution for salvation because ....
    who has given it the mission of .... (73)
2. The Church is not of this world, but it ...., and tries
    to be seen by the world as .... and as .... (74)

B. BIBLE READING   John 21, 15-23

The Primacy Given to Peter

After they had finished eating, Jesus said to Peter, "Simon, son of John, do you love me more than these others do?"

Peter answered, "Yes, Lord, you know I love you."

"Feed my lambs," said Jesus. Then he asked again, "Simon, son of John, do you love me?"

He replied, "Yes, Lord, you know I love you."

Again Jesus said to him, "Look after my sheep."

Then the third time Jesus said, "Simon, son of John, do you love me?"

Peter felt very bad that Jesus should ask that question three times. He knew that Jesus was thinking of the three times that he had denied Him on the night of His trial. He answered, "Lord, you know everything; you know I love you."

Jesus said to him, "Feed my sheep."

Jesus did know that Peter loved him. But he wanted to remind him that he had a work for Peter to do, a work which would demand the sacrifice of his life.

Jesus continued, "When you were a young man, Peter, you used to fasten your own belt and go wherever you wished. But when you grow old, you will stretch out your hands, and another will fasten a belt around you and take you where you do not wish to go."

In these words Jesus indicated the kind of death by which Peter would give glory to God, that is, by being crucified.

Then Jesus said to him, "You must follow me."

Peter turned round and noticed John following behind them. So he said, "Yes, Lord, but what about him?"

"If it is my wish," replied Jesus, "for him to stay until I come, is that your business, Peter? You must follow me."

Till now Peter had only received the promise of the primacy, but after this morning meal Jesus conferred the primacy upon him in all the fullness and majesty in the presence of the other apostles. It was truly divine power—divine in its origin and nature for it represents Jesus: "Feed my lambs"; divine in its extent, for it embraces the whole Church, the hearing (the lambs) as well as the teaching body (the sheep), and includes the entire and supreme power; divine in its operation and significance, for the whole Church—its being, attributes, stability, life, growth, and work—stands and falls with the primacy. Always the Church will feed the sheep and lambs, without distinction and without exception, on holy doctrine.

When Jesus was about to leave his sheep, he appointed Peter the shepherd in his place. As a shepherd, Peter would have his chance to lay down his life. As a youth he had been his own master; but in his old age, his hands would be stretched on the cross. Peter was crucified on Vatican hill in Rome about the year 67.

Discussion:

1. What did Jesus ask Peter?

2. What did Jesus ask Peter to do as a proof of his love?

3. How did Jesus describe Peter's death?

4. What did Jesus have to say about John?

5. What kind of power did Jesus bestow on Peter?

6. When and where did Peter die?

C. PRACTICE

1. The people who belong to a parish are members of Christ's kingdom. Their duty is to work with the pastor in the whole life of the parish. They are to take an active part in the worship, belong to and work together in various parish organizations, support the parish financially, and carry the teaching and sanctifying action of the Church into the community in which they live and work. Since the parish is Christ in the community, its duty is to care for the members of the parish and to go out in search of those who have strayed from the practice of their faith, and of those who do not yet share the fullness of the Mystical Body of Christ.

2. It is the duty of Catholics to be mission-minded. All men are meant to be incorporated into the Body of Christ, the Church,

because he died for all. Catholics can help the foreign and home missions not only by their generous contributions, but also by their prayers and their zeal in promoting interest in the work of the missions.

JESUS SPEAKS:

"I assure you, as often as you did it for one of my least brothers, you did it for me."   (Mt 25, 40)

"Whoever welcomes a child such as this for my sake welcomes me. And whoever welcomes me welcomes, not me, but him who sent me."   (Mk 9, 37)

"Any man who gives you a drink of water because you belong to Christ will not, I assure you, go without his reward." (Mk 9, 41)

"Anyone among you who aspires to greatness must serve the rest, and whoever wants to rank first among you must serve the needs of all."   (Mt 20, 26. 27)

"Full authority has been given to me both in heaven and on earth; go, therefore, and make disciples of all the nations. Baptize them in the name 'of the Father, and of the Son, and of the Holy Spirit.' Teach them to carry out everything I have commanded you. And know that I am with you always, until the end of the world!"   (Mt 28, 18-20)

Sacraments are seven streams of Grace from the Cross

Part Six — THE SACRAMENTS

CHAPTER

14

The Sacraments, Actions of Christ in the Church

75. **How is the saving work of Christ continued in the Church?**

Through the gift of the Holy Spirit, the Church (1) enjoys the presence of Christ (2) and carries on his ministry and saving mission.

(1) Before ascending into heaven, Jesus gave his apostles a command to teach all nations and to baptize them. He promised to be with them. "Teach them to carry out everything I have commanded you. And know that I am with you always, until the end of the world!" (Mt 28, 20).

Jesus is with his Church also through the gift of the Holy Spirit. He promised this the night before he died. "If I fail to go, the Paraclete will never come to you, whereas if I go, I will send him to you" (Jn 16, 7).

(2) Through the Holy Spirit the Church is able to carry on the work of salvation given to it by Christ.

76. What means does Church have for carrying on Christ's work? ....

The Church has been given special means for carrying on Christ's work, namely, the sacraments which he instituted.

Christ's work of salvation is continued in the Church especially in the sacraments. The sacraments are special actions in the Church through which the life of God is given to his people.

77. What are the sacraments?

The sacraments are outward signs both of God's grace and man's faith.

The sacraments are signs that we can see, which let us know that God's grace is being given to the soul of the person who receives the sacrament. We can see the signs with our bodily eyes, but it is only through faith that we know God's grace is given to us. We believe this on the word of Jesus himself who gave us the sacraments to make it possible for us to share God's own life, through grace. This grace helps us to worship God and to love God and our neighbor.

In the sacraments the words together with the action make up the sacred sign. Water, since it is so necessary for life, can be used as a sign of life—a sign also of divine life in baptism. Oil is used to strengthen and heal the body. It is used in confirmation to show the strength we receive from this sacrament and to give us that strength. Baptism not only signifies life, it really produces it. Confirmation not only signifies strength but gives it. Anointing of the sick is not only a sign of health but gives it to the soul and body.

78. What do the sacraments show?

The sacraments show (1) that God wants to make man holy (2) and that man wants to receive this holiness. In this way the sacraments bring us God's grace.

(1) The sacraments are the signs that Christ began, which show us that grace is being given and that they themselves produce this grace. God gave us the sacraments in order to show that he wants us to be made holy by giving us his grace. By grace we share in the very life of God himself, for through baptism we are born again. God lives in us as in a temple. We are truly children of God through grace. All this happens when Jesus comes to us in the sacraments.

(2) We show that we are willing to receive Christ's grace if we often and earnestly receive the sacraments.

79. Why are the sacraments called actions of Christ?

Sacraments are called actions of Christ (1) because through them he gives his Spirit to Christians and makes them a holy people, (2) and because from Christ they get their power to make us holy.

(1) In the sacraments Christ gives us his grace, bought for us on the cross, to help us to become more like him. The Church is the community of those whom God has called to give witness to his Son Jesus and to the new life he has brought to man. In this community of the People of God the Holy Spirit gives and strengthens the life of God through the sacraments, prayers, and works of service for others.

(2) The Church has the power of administering the sacraments, but the Church receives this power from Christ. It is Christ who baptizes, who forgives sins. It is not so much a man who celebrates the Eucharist as Christ himself, for he offers himself in the Sacrifice of the Mass by the ministry of the priests. The action of the sacrament is the action of Christ. The priests who administer the sacraments are only ordained representatives of Christ, our high priest, and his instruments.

80. **What is the purpose of the sacraments?**

The purpose of the sacraments is (1) to make men holy, (2) to build up the body of Christ, the Church, (3) and to give worship to God.

(1) The sacraments are the ordinary channels of God's grace and are necessary to keep the life of grace in our soul. Jesus gives us his grace to make us holy.

(2) Each of the sacraments plays an important part in the life of the Church. They give us the grace we need to become living members of the Body of Christ, which is the Church. Thus the Body of Christ grows.

(3) By means of the Eucharist Christ reoffers himself to the Father through the ministry of his priest in the Sacrifice of the Mass. This is the greatest act of worship that can be given to God. At Mass Jesus and the faithful daily adore the Father. With him they give glory to God and praise him for his mercy and generosity toward mankind. This we do in a manner worthy of God.

81. **Why does the Church urge Catholics to receive the sacraments?**

The Church urges Catholics to receive the sacraments (1) often and with great eagerness, because the sacraments were instituted to nourish Christian life; (2) and with faith because they are sacraments of faith.

(1) Christ made the sacraments instruments to produce grace in us. In order that the faithful may nourish their Christian life, the Church urges all Catholics not only to understand the meaning of all the sacraments, but to receive them eagerly and frequently. (2) The more faith and love we have when we receive the sacraments, the more grace they will give us. We must not neglect to use the means God has given us to grow holy and pleasing to him by sharing his divine life.

82. **What are the effects of the sacraments?**

The sacraments are (1) sources of grace for individuals and communities; (2) remedies for sin and the effects of sin.

(1) Jesus Christ is the source of divine life. He gives us this life and increases it within us by means of the seven channels of grace which are called the sacraments. Through the sacraments Christ is with us throughout our lives to provide us with all the help and strength we need to grow in the divine life. He is always there to forgive us, to nourish us, and to prepare us for the vocation in which we serve him in the Church.

A sacrament is a sacred sign instituted by Christ to give grace. This grace is given for the benefit of the person who receives the sacrament and also for the benefit of the whole community of believers. The sacraments are instruments of divine life for the family of God.

(2) Mortal sin is the greatest evil in the world because it drives out of our soul the divine life of sanctifying grace and turns us away from God, the source of all life, peace, and joy. But our Lord protects our soul from serious sin by giving us more sanctifying grace in the sacraments, especially in Holy Communion. In addition each sacrament gives its own particular actual or sacramental graces and a right to future actual graces. These sacramental graces give us the light to see what is evil and the strength we need to fight against it. In this way our soul is strengthened against temptation. This is especially true of Holy Communion which is a remedy for our spiritual sickness and weakness.

Teacher reference: Principal Elements, no. 97

A. FILL IN THE BLANKS

1. Through the gift of the Holy Spirit (1) the Church enjoys .... (2) and carries on .... (75)

2. The special means for carrying on Christ's work are .... (76)

3. The sacraments are .... both of .... and
   .... (77)

4. The sacraments show thaat God wants .... (78)

5. Sacraments are called actions of Christ because ....
   and .... (79)

6. The purpose of the sacraments is (1) to ....
   (2) to .... (3) and to .... (80)

7. The Church urges Catholics to receive the sacraments often
   and with great eagerness because .... (81)

8. The Church urges Catholics to receive the sacraments with
   faith because .... (81)

9. The sacraments are sources of grace for .... (82)

10. The sacraments are remedies for .... (82)

B. BIBLE READING

John 4, 4-42

The Samaritan Woman

One morning, Jesus stopped to rest beside an old well at the foot of a mountain. His disciples had gone to the village to buy food.

Just at this moment a Samaritan woman came to the well with her water jar upon her head. Jesus said to her, "Please give me a drink."

She said to him, "How is it that you, who are a Jew, ask a drink of me, a Samaritan woman?"

Jesus answered, "If you knew the gift of God, and who asks you for a drink, you would have asked of him, and he would have given you living water."

The woman said, "Sir, you have nothing to draw with, and the well is deep. From where, then, do you have living water?"

"Whoever drinks of this water," said Jesus, "shall thirst again; but whoever drinks of the water that I shall give him, shall never thirst."

"Sir," said the woman, "give me some of this water that I may not thirst, or come here to draw water."

Jesus told her the sins that she had committed. Much surprised, she said, "Sir, I see that you are a prophet. I know that when the Messiah comes, he will tell us all things."

Jesus said, "I who speak with you am he."

Just at this time the disciples of Jesus came back from the village. Jesus said to them, "My food is to do the will of him who sent me, to accomplish his work."

When the Samaritan woman went to the town, she said to the people, "Come and see a man who has told me all that I have ever done. Can he be the Christ?"

Jesus said to the Women, "I am the Christ."

Soon the woman came back to the well with many of her people. They asked Jesus to come to their town and to stay there and teach them. He went with them and stayed two days. Many of the people believed in Jesus and said, "We have heard for ourselves; now we know that this is indeed the Savior of the world."

Discussion:

1. What did Jesus say about the living water he gives those who come to him?
2. What did Jesus answer to the woman when she mentioned the Messiah?
3. What did Jesus tell his disciples when they returned from the village?
4. How did the woman get the people to come to Jesus?
5. What did the people say about Jesus after he stayed with them two days?
6. How does Jesus give us this "living water" through the sacraments?

C. PRACTICE

1. The more faith and love we have when we receive the sacraments, the more grace they will give us. It is true that the sacraments worthily received always give grace, even if they are received without enough preparation. But it is also true that the better prepared we are to receive them the more grace we will receive. We should, therefore, receive the sacraments with great devotion.

2. The sacrament of the Eucharist and the sacrament of penance are the sacraments we can receive most frequently. We should try to receive the Eucharist every Sunday or Saturday evening, and even as often as we can during the week. It would be good to receive the sacrament of penance at least each month in order to obtain the graces we need to lead a good Christian life.

JESUS SPEAKS:

"Live on in me, as I do in you. No more than a branch can bear fruit of itself apart from the vine, can you bear fruit apart from me." (Jn 15, 4)

"I am the vine, you are the branches. He who lives in me and I in him, will produce abundantly, for apart from me you can do nothing" (Jn 15, 5)

In Penance
Jesus takes
away my sins

CHAPTER
15

Instruction
on the Sacraments

83. **What is baptism?**

Baptism is the sacrament (1) of rebirth as a child of God made holy by the Spirit, (2) of unity with Jesus in his death and resurrection, (3) of cleansing from original and personal sins, (4) and of welcome into the community of the Church.

(1) Baptism is a new birth as a child of God, a beginning of a new life in us, which is God's own life of grace brought to us by Jesus Christ. Jesus himself baptizes and makes us holy with the gifts of the Holy Spirit and impresses on our soul a character that cannot be taken away.

Three of the sacraments, baptism, confirmation and holy orders, produce in the soul a mark which can never be lost. This mark, which is called a character, is a kind of badge of our membership in Christ, a sharing in his eternal priesthood, by which we are dedicated to sacred worship. These sacraments may be received only once.

(2) Baptism unites the new Christian so closely to Jesus that he shares in his death and resurrection. Through this sacrament he dies to his old self, that is, his life of sin, and rises to new life, a life of grace.

(3) The result of baptism is that a person is brought to peace with God: his sins are forgiven, he receives the life of God.

(4) A person enters the Church by a new birth in baptism. He becomes part of God's People. He needs the company of his fellow Christians as he grows in faith and shares in the continuing work of Jesus in the world.

84. What is confirmation?

Confirmation is the sacrament by which those born again in baptism now receive the seal of the Holy Spirit, the gift of the Father and the Son.

Confirmation strengthens the life of the Spirit received at baptism. Jesus sends the Holy Spirit once more to the Christian souls with new grace and new strength to lead the Christian life. The sign of confirmation is made by the bishop as he extends his hands over the confirmed and prays that the Holy Spirit come upon them. This seal of the Spirit is the gift of the Father and the Son.

85. What does the seal of the Spirit do for us?

The seal of the Spirit prepares us (1) to be witnesses of Christ by a mature Christian life, (2) and to spread and defend the faith while living in the world.

(1) Confirmation unites the Christian more perfectly to the Church and gives him the special strength of the Holy Spirit. This strength helps him to live in the world as a witness of Christ and to serve his fellow men.

(2) A duty was placed upon us when we were confirmed: to bring Jesus Christ, his example, his way of life, and his Church to others. The strength of the grace of the Holy Spirit will help us to do so if we are generous enough to show some effort and to ask for his help in prayer.

Teacher reference:
Worshiping Community, no. 117

86. What is penance?

Penance is the sacrament which brings to the Christian God's merciful forgiveness for sins committed after baptism.

In the sacrament of penance Jesus comes to forgive the sins of a baptized Christian bringing the sinner consolation and peace.

Jesus gave the power of forgiving sins to his apostles when he appeared to them the evening of the day of his resurrection. " 'Peace be with you,' he said again. 'As the Father has sent me, so I send you." Then he breathed on them and said: "Receive the Holy Spirit. If you forgive men's sins, they are forgiven them; if you hold them bound, they are held bound' " (Jn 20, 20-23).

87. What are the effects of penance?

Penance is (1) a means of obtaining pardon from God after a sincere confession, true sorrow, and the will not to sin again. (2) It brings about peace with the Church, which is wounded by our sins. (3) It helps us to work for holiness of life and to overcome habits of sin.

(1) The sacrament of penance is the means God gave us of his forgiveness for our sins. But we must be truly sorry for our sins, confess them to a priest, and receive absolution from the priest. We then do penance by saying the prayers or doing the good deeds assigned by the priest in confession. The sign of the sacrament can be seen when the sinner shows sorrow for sin, confesses his sins, and is willing to do penance for them, and when the priest says, "I absolve you from your sins in the name of the Father, and of the Son, and of the Holy Spirit."

(2) The sacrament of penance also brings about peace with the Church, which we have hurt by our sins.

(3) Through the sacrament of penance Jesus, the Good Shepherd, forgives our sins and sends his Holy Spirit once more to our

soul with new grace and new strength to lead a better Christian life. We can join ourselves to Jesus, dying to sin and selfishness and rising with him to new life with God. Only with his help can we overcome temptation and avoid sin. Only with his grace can we practice virtue and become more like Jesus.

88. **Is confession necessary if one has fallen into serious sin?**

If one has fallen into serious sin, sacramental confession is the ordinary way established in the Church to bring about peace between the sinner and Christ and his Church.

Repentance and forgiveness of sins committed after baptism are expressed in the Church through the sacrament of penance. It is the ordinary way offered by the Church to bring about peace with Christ and his Church. Since the life of Christians is filled with temptations and sins, this sacrament is open for them so that they may obtain pardon from the merciful God.

89. **What is the effect of perfect sorrow for sin?**

A sinner can also be restored to grace by perfect sorrow (contrition) for sin because he has offended God.

We have sorrow or contrition for our sins when we are sorry for them because they have offended the good God, our Father, and when we do not want to commit them again. Our sorrow is sincere when it comes from the heart. The real meaning of the virtue of penance is hatred for sin as an offense against God who is all-good and worthy of our love.

We should have contrition for mortal sin because it offends God seriously and keeps us from reaching heaven. It condemns us to eternal punishment. By true sorrow we can be forgiven and receive God's grace again.

90. What is the wish of the Church concerning confession?

Every Catholic, from his early years, should be instructed how to receive and best profit from the regular use of this sacrament.

The Church urges us to confess our sins with sincere sorrow in the sacrament of penance. It wishes us to use frequently those sacraments which help us to live a better Christian ilfe, and the sacrament of penance is one of them. After the Eucharist, it is the one that can be received most frequently.

Teacher reference: Principal Elements, nos. 99, 123, 124

91. What is holy orders?

Holy orders (1) makes certain members of the People of God like Christ the Mediator, (2) puts them in positions of special service in the Church (3) and gives them a sacred power to carry out this service.

(1) Christ is the Mediator between us and the Father through his priesthood. He continues his sacrifice of the cross in the Church at Holy Mass through his priests.

(2) Through this sacrament Jesus shares the work of his priesthood with other men—the bishops and the priests of the Catholic Church. Through them he makes himself present to offer the sacrifice of the Mass, to baptize, to give the sacrament of confirmation, to give his Body and Blood in Holy Communion, to forgive sins in the sacrament of penance, to anoint the sick, and to bless marriages. The major orders of the Church are deacon, priest, and bishop.

(3) By his own authority Jesus appointed the apostles to be his priests to carry on his work in the world. At the Last Supper he gave the apostles the power to change bread and wine into his Body and Blood in memory of him. After his resurrection he gave them the power to forgive men's sins. Before ascending into heaven he sent them to all nations to teach and baptize.

92. **What special grace does Christ give in the sacrament of holy orders?**

Through this sacrament Christ gives the special grace of the Holy Spirit (1) to guide and take care of those who believe, (2) to proclaim and explain the gospel, (3) and to guide and sanctify God's people.

(1) Before he ascended into heaven, Jesus gave special instructions to his apostles. He wanted to be sure that there would be helpers to take care of his flock.

(2) Jesus sent his apostles to preach the gospel of the New Covenant to every nation because he wanted to save all men.

(3) The apostles continued Christ's priestly work of being mediators between God and man. They brought God's mercy and grace to the people and, in return, gave man's praise to God. Christ was present, acting through them.

93. **What can priests do as Christ's representatives?**

Representing Christ, priests (1) offer the Sacrifice of the Mass and (2) administer the sacrament of penance for the forgiveness of sins, (3) and the sacrament of the anointing of the sick.

(1) Knowing that the priesthood of Jesus and his Church was to be continued to the end of time, the apostles by ordaining priests and bishops passed on their priestly power to others. The most important work of the priest is the offering of the Sacrifice of the Mass. He acts in the name of Christ and in union with him as Jesus renews the sacrifice of the cross in an unbloody way for the glory of God and the salvation of all men.

(2) Through his priests Jesus forgives our sins and becomes, for all of us, a merciful high priest.

(3) Through his priests Jesus gives comfort to the suffering members of the Church and prepares them for their eternal union with God.

Teacher reference: Worshiping Community, no. 132

94. What is the anointing of the sick?

The anointing of the sick is the sacrament for the seriously ill, infirm and aged.

Jesus showed a great love for sinners and the sick. He gave special care to the sick and cured them. He continues to come to the sick in the sacrament of the anointing of the sick. The sign of this sacrament is the anointing with oil and the words of the priest. The priest anoints the eyes, ears, nose, lips, hands, and sometimes the feet of the sick person.

95. When is this sacrament best received?

This sacrament is best received as soon as the danger of death begins, from sickness or old age.

This sacrament is for those who are seriously sick. The sacrament can be repeated for persons who get well and become seriously ill again. Sorrow for sins is required to have sins forgiven.

96. What does the Church ask for by this Anointing?

(1) By this anointing and prayers for health, the Church through the priests asks the Lord (2) to lighten the sufferings of the sick, (3) forgive their sins, (4) and bring them to eternal salvation.

(1) Jesus comes to the sick in this sacrament and it may restore the sick person to health.

(2) Jesus gives graces to the sick which help them to bear the pain of their illness with patience.

(3) Jesus gives graces that help the sick to have deep sorrow for their sins, and this is needed for forgiveness.

(4) By this sacrament the sick or aged are prepared for entrance into the glory of heaven.

97. What does the Church encourage the sick to do?

The Church encourages the sick to help the People of God by offering their sufferings with the sufferings and death of Jesus.

Since Jesus gives us his grace and divine life in this sacrament, he helps us to offer our sufferings in union with his own on the cross that we might share in the work of the redemption. In this way we can help the Church not only by making up for sin, but also by meriting grace for the Church. If we share in the sufferings of Jesus, we can expect to share also in his glory.

Before the sacrament of the anointing of the sick the priest usually gives the sick person the sacrament of penance. After the anointing he gives the Body and Blood of Christ.

Teacher reference: Worshiping Community, no. 127

A. FILL IN THE BLANKS

1. Baptism is the sacrament (1) of ....
made holy by ...., (2) of unity with Jesus in
...................................., (3) of cleansing from..........................,
(4) and of welcome into .... (83)

2. Confirmation is the sacrament by which ....
now receive ...., the gift of .... (84)

3. The seal of the Spirit prepares us (1) to be .... by a
mature ...., (2) and to .... while
living in the world. (85)

4. Penance is the sacrament which brings to the Christian ....
............................for sins committed .... (86)

5. Penance is a means of .... after .... (86)

6. Penance brings about ...., which is wounded by ....
and it helps us .... and to .... (87)

7. If one has fallen into serious sin, sacramental confession is
.... to bring about .... (88)

8. A sinner can also be restored to grace ....
because he has .... (89)

9. Every Catholic, from his early years, should be instructed
.... and .... from the ....
of the sacrament of penance. (90)

10. Holy orders (1) makes certain members of the People of God
...........................; (2) puts them in positions ....
in the Church (3) and gives them .... (91)

11. Through the sacrament of holy orders Christ gives ....
(1) to .... (2) to .... (3) and to
.... (92)

12. Representing Christ, priests (1) offer ...., and
(2) administer the sacrament of .... (3)
and the sacrament of .... (93)

13. The anointing of the sick is .... (94)

14. The anointing of the sick is best received ....
from .... (95)

15. (1) By the anointing and prayers the Church asks the Lord for
.... (2) to lighten .... (3) to forgive ....
(4) and bring them to .... (96)

16. The Church encourages the sick to .... by
offering their sufferings with .... (97)

B. BIBLE READING   John 20, 19-23
Appearance to the Disciples

On the evening of the first day of the week, the day on which Jesus rose from the dead, Jesus came to visit his disciples. Even though they had locked the doors of the place where they were for fear of the Jews, Jesus came and stood before them.

"Peace be with you," he said.

When he had said this, he showed them his hands and his side. At the sight of the Lord the disciples rejoiced.

"Peace be with you," he said again. "As the Father has sent me, so I send you."

Then he breathed on them and said: "Receive the Holy Spirit. If you forgive men's sins, they are forgiven them; if you hold them bound, they are held bound."

Discussion:

1. Why did the disciples lock the door after Jesus died?
2. How did the disciples feel when they saw Jesus?
3. How did Jesus greet his disciples?
4. What did Jesus say to his disciples?
5. Why did Jesus breathe on them?
6. What power did Jesus give his apostles?
7. How is this power used today?

C. PRACTICE

1. We should often ask the Holy Spirit to give us the graces offered us through our confirmation, especially the grace to overcome temptation to sin, and the grace to be a good example in living our Christian faith so that we may be witnesses of Christ in the world.

2. We should examine our conscience every day. Just before retiring at night we should make an effort to recall the sins we have committed during the day, and then make an act of contrition for these as well as all our past sins.

3. The Church wishes us to use the sacrament of penance frequently once each month, or oftener if we can, so that we may overcome our habits of sin and receive the grace we need to live a better Christian life.

JESUS SPEAKS:

" 'Peace' is my farewell to you, my peace is my gift to you; I do not give it to you as the world gives peace."   (Jn 14, 27)

Jesus is my
Food in
Holy Communion

16   The Holy Eucharist

98. Why is the Eucharist the center of all sacramental life?

The Eucharist is the center of all sacramental life because it is of the greatest importance for uniting and strengthening the Church.

Of all the sacraments, the most important is the sacrament of the Eucharist. Jesus Christ is present in the Holy Eucharist to be our sacrifice, our food, our life, our companion to strengthen and nourish us with his flesh and blood. He comes to us to unite us with himself and with all the members of the Church.

99. Why is the Eucharistic celebration carried out?

The Eucharistic celebration is carried out in obedience to the words of Jesus at the Last Supper: "Do this in memory of me."

At the Last Supper Jesus gave bread and wine to his apostles to eat and drink, telling them that it was his own Body and Blood. He then asked them to remember him always by doing this same thing among themselves.

The Mass is the Church's way of doing what Jesus did at the Last Supper. Jesus gave the apostles the command and the power to bring the Eucharist to us when he said, "Do this in memory of me."

100. What happens when a priest speaks the words of Eucharistic consecration?

When a priest pronounces the words of Eucharistic consecration, the bread and wine is changed into the Body and Blood of Christ, given in sacrifice.

His words and power made Jesus really present in the bread and wine that he gave his apostles to eat. They actually received Jesus in that meal and were united with him. This made the apostles one with Jesus and all he did. They shared his gift of himself to his Father on the cross, for he was given in sacrifice. The apostles then gave Christ to the People of God in the Eucharist.

101. How is Christ present in the Eucharist?

Christ himself, true God and true man, is really and substantially present, in a mysterious way, under the appearances of bread and wine.

When Jesus gave the apostles his Body, the Body looked like bread and even tasted like bread but it was not bread; it was his Body for he said so. When he gave the apostles his Blood, the Blood appeared to be wine and even tasted like wine, but it was not wine; it was his Blood for he said so. This holy sacrament looks like bread and tastes like bread but it is not bread; it is Jesus. To come to us Jesus covers himself with the appearances of bread and wine. We cannot understand this, but we take the word of God that it is so. The Eucharist is called the Mystery of Faith.

All priests in the Catholic Church have the power to change bread and wine into Christ. In the Eucharist it is Christ himself who consecrates through the priest as the words of consecration are said: "This is my body. This cup is the new covenant in my blood."

102. What is the Sacrifice of the Mass?

(1) The Sacrifice of the Mass is not only a ritual which reminds us of the sacrifice of Calvary. (2) In it, through the ministry of priests, Christ continues till the end of time the sacrifice of the cross in an unbloody manner.

(1) At the Last Supper, Jesus instituted the Eucharist sacrifice of his Body and Blood to continue for all time the sacrifice of the cross until he would come again. He gave his Church a remembrance of his death and resurrection.

(2) But the Mass is also a true sacrifice. Through the hands of priests and in the name of the whole Church, the sacrifice of Jesus is offered in the Eucharist in an unbloody and sacramental way. The priest, by the sacred power he receives from Christ, and acting in the person of Christ, brings about the Eucharistic sacrifice, and offers it to God in the name of all the people.

The Mass is a sacrifice where the Church not only remembers Jesus but really brings him and his saving death and resurrection into the present so that his followers may become part of it. When the Church celebrates the Eucharist, Jesus is really there. It is he who does once more what he did at the Last Supper.

103. What is Holy Communion?

The Eucharist is also a meal which (1) reminds us of the Last Supper, (2) celebrates our unity together in Christ, (3) and already now makes present the messianic banquet of the kingdom of heaven.

(1) Jesus nourishes our soul with himself, the Bread of Life. He offered himself as a sacrifice on the cross. In Holy Communion we partake of the Body that was given in death for us, the Blood

that was shed for our salvation. This holy meal reminds us of what happened at the Last Supper when Jesus told his apostles to do this in memory of him.

(2) The Communion of the Mass is the meal of the Lord's Body that nourishes us with the life of God and unites us to Jesus and to one another. In drawing us to union with Jesus, our heavenly Father draws us closer to each other because we share in the divine life of Jesus through his grace. The Holy Eucharist is not only a sign of the unity and love that binds us to Jesus and each other, but it gives us the grace we need to make that love strong and sincere.

(3) Holy Communion is already giving us a part of the banquet of Christ in the kingdom of heaven because it is the same Son of God made man who will be united with us in a union of joy forever in heaven. Jesus also promised that our body would some day enjoy his presence. He said, "He who feeds on my flesh and drinks my blood has life eternal, and I will raise him up on the last day" (Jn 6, 54). The meal, prepared for us by God the Father, makes us ready to take part in that heavenly communion with Jesus and his Father.

104. **What does Jesus do for Christians in the Eucharist?**
In the Eucharist Jesus nourishes Christians with his own self, the Bread of Life, so that they may become a people more pleasing to God and filled with greater love of God and neighbor.

Holy Communion is Jesus Christ himself under the appearances of bread and wine uniting himself to the Christian to nourish his soul. Jesus said, "I myself am the living bread come down from heaven. If anyone eats this bread he shall live forever; the bread I will give is my flesh, for the life of the world" (Jn 6, 51).

Holy Communion helps us to love God more because of the divine grace which grows in our souls. This same grace helps us to love others for the love of God. Jesus strengthens us through actual or sacramental grace that we may overcome temptation and avoid sinning against God and our neighbor. Only by the help of his grace can we truly live a life of charity and fulfill his greatest commandment.

105. What must we do to receive the Eucharist worthily?

To receive the Eucharist worthily we must be in the state of grace.

As long as we are in the state of grace, we are prepared to receive Jesus each time that we are present at the Holy Sacrifice of the Mass, because his Body, the food of this sacrificial meal, is for us the way to eternal life. The best way to prepare our soul for union with Jesus in Holy Communion is to offer him and to offer ourselves with him to God the Father in the Sacrifice of the Mass. Confession is not necessary before Holy Communion unless we have a serious sin to confess, but we should receive the sacrament of penance faithfully, each month or oftener, if we wish.

106. Why is the Eucharist a sacrament of unity?

The Eucharist is a sacrament of unity because it unites the faithful more closely with God and with one another.

By eating the Body of the Lord, we are taken up into a close union with him and with one another. St. Paul said, "Because the loaf of bread is one, we, many though we are, are one body, for we all partake of the one loaf" (1 Cor 10, 17).

107. Why is the Eucharist reserved in our churches?

The Eucharist is reserved in our churches to be a powerful help to prayer and the service of others.

Reservation of the Blessed Sacrament means that at the end of Communion the remaining Consecrated Bread is placed in the tabernacle and reverently reserved. The Eucharist reserved is a continuing sign of our Lord's real presence among his people and spiritual food for the sick and dying.

108. **What do we owe Christ in the Blessed Sacrament reserved?**

We owe gratitude, adoration, and devotion to the real presence of Christ in the Blessed Sacrament reserved.

We must show gratitude, adoration, and devotion to the real presence of Christ. We show this devotion in our visits to the tabernacle in our churches and in Benediction. Benediction is a brief ceremony in which the Blessed Sacrament is exposed to the people for reverence and adoration. The priest blesses the people with the Lord's Body.

Teacher reference:
Catechesis for a Worshiping Community, no. 120

A. FILL IN THE BLANKS

1. The Eucharist is the center of .... because it is of the greatest importance for .... (98)
2. The Eucharistic celebration is carried out in obedience to .... (99)
3. When a priest pronounces the words of Eucharistic consecration, the bread and wine .... (100)
4. Christ himself, true God and true man, is .... present, in a mysterious way, under the appearances of .... (101)
5. (1) The sacrifice of the Mass is not only a .... (2) In it, through the ministry .... Christ continues till the end of time .... (102)
6. The Eucharist is also a .... (1) which reminds us of ...., (2) celebrates ...., (3) and already now makes present .... of the kingdom of heaven. (103)
7. In the Eucharist Jesus nourishes Christians with ...., so that they may become .... and filled with .... (104)
8. To receive the Eucharist worthily we must .... (105)

9. The Eucharist is a sacrament of unity because .... (106)
10. The Eucharist is reserved in our churches to be a powerful help .... (107)
11. We owe .... to the real presence of Christ in the Blessed Sacrament reserved. (108)

B. BIBLE READING   The Promise of the Holy Eucharist
John 6, 48-69

Jesus came again to Capernaum and went into the synagogue, which was full of people, some of whom had eaten of the five loaves. These people wanted Jesus to feed them in the same way again, but he said to them, "You seek me because you have eaten of the loaves. Do not labor for the food that perishes, but for that which endures unto life everlasting, which the Son of Man will give you."

They said to him, "Lord, give us always this bread."

But he answered, "I myself am the living bread come down from heaven. If anyone eats this bread he shall live forever; the bread that I will give is my flesh, for the life of the world."

The Jews argued with one another, saying, "How can he give us his flesh to eat?"

Our Lord did not change the meaning of his words. Instead he said what he meant with even stronger words, "I solemnly assure you, if you do not eat the flesh of the Son of Man and drink his blood, you shall not have life in you. He who feeds on my flesh and drinks my blood has life eternal, and I will raise him up on the last day. For my flesh is real food and my blood real drink. The man who feeds on my flesh and drinks my blood remains in me, and I in him."

When the people heard this, many of them said, "This sort of talk is hard to endure! How can anyone take it seriously?" And they began to depart.

Jesus then turned to his apostles and asked, "Does it shake your faith? Do you want to leave me too?"

Simon Peter answered him, "Lord, to whom shall we go? You have the words of eternal life. We have come to believe; we are convinced that you are God's holy one."

Discussion:

1. What did Jesus say about himself as the living bread from heaven.
2. Why did the Jews argue over the words of Jesus?
3. What did Jesus say in answer to the Jews?
4. Why did the Jews begin to depart?
5. What did Peter say when Jesus asked him whether he wanted to leave him or not?
6. What do the words of Jesus on the Eucharist tell us about Holy Communion?

The Institution of the Eucharist   Mt 26, 26-28

When it was evening, Jesus with his twelve Apostles went to the house which Peter and John had found for the Passover meal. In the upper room he sat down with them to eat the Passover. This Thursday night was our Lord's last night on earth before his death. He said, "I have longed to eat this Passover with you before I suffer."

During the supper Jesus told his Apostles many important things. He gave them his own commandment of love for one another; he promised to send them the Holy Spirit; he asked them to remain united with him; he prayed to his Father for them. But most of all, he gave us the Holy Eucharist by instituting the Sacrifice of the Mass.

The Last Supper

As they were eating, Jesus took some bread, and when he had said the blessing, he broke it and gave it to the disciples. "Take this and eat it," he said, "this is my body." Then he took a cup, gave thanks, and gave it to them. "All of you must drink from it," he said, "for this is my blood, the blood of the covenant, to be poured out in behalf of many for the forgiveness of sins. Do this in remembrance of me."

The Eucharist is a memorial of our Lord's Passion and Death. This Flesh which he gave to his Apostles to eat was the Flesh of the sacrificial Victim who would offer himself on the cross; this Blood was the Blood that was to be shed for our redemption on Calvary. By giving us the Mass, Jesus made it possible for us to be present at the Sacrifice of Calvary, which is now reenacted on the altar in an unbloody manner. In Holy Communion we receive the Victim of Calvary as food for the nourishment of our souls. Jesus left this Gift of himself for the end as his death-bed Gift of love. We must love him in return by appreciating the Mass and Holy Communion.

Discussion:

1. Where did Jesus go for the Passover meal?
2. When did Jesus institute the Blessed Sacrament of the Altar?
3. What did Jesus do at the Last Supper?
4. Why is the Eucharist a memorial of our Lord's Passion and Death?
5. Why is the Mass the same sacrifice which Jesus offered on the cross?
6. How must we show our love for the Holy Eucharist?

C. PRACTICE

1. The people at the time of our Lord could see his face, could hear his voice, could feel the touch of his hand as he blessed them. Though we cannot see him with the eyes of the body, we have the greater privilege of receiving his sacred body, of eating his flesh and drinking his blood. By means of the Holy Eucharist, his greatest gift to us, we have his lasting presence among us. We should share in the sacrificial meal of Holy Communion at least each Sunday, and during the week if we can, so that we may grow in the love of Christ and in his grace.

2. When, for some reason, we are unable to receive Holy Communion we should make a "spiritual communion" any time of the day, that is, desire to be united with Jesus in sincere love.

We share Christ's life together in the Family

CHAPTER

17 The Sacrament of Matrimony

109. Who instituted marriage?

Marriage was instituted by the Creator himself and given by him certain purposes, laws, and blessings.

At the very beginning of the human race, when he created Adam and Eve, God instituted marriage. We read in the Book of Genesis: "God created man in his image; in the divine image he created him; male and female he created them. God blessed them, saying: 'Be fertile and multiply; fill the earth and subdue it'" (Gn 1, 27-28).

110. Who raised marriage to the dignity of a sacrament?

Christ raised marriage of the baptized to the dignity of a sacrament.

Jesus Christ made marriage a lifelong, sacred union of husband and wife by which they give themselves to each other and to him. He raised this union to the dignity of a sacrament for the baptized.

111. Who are the ministers of the sacrament?

The spouses, expressing their personal and lasting consent, are the ministers of the sacrament.

The husband is the minister of God's grace to the wife and the wife to the husband. The priest officiates at the ceremony as the Church's witness to this act of grace.

112. In what do we see the dignity of the sacrament?

(1) The spouses live together in Christ's grace; (2) they imitate Christ's own love for his Church; (3) they are consecrated to live up to the dignity of matrimony and to carry out its duties.

(1) In the sacrament of matrimony Christ comes to man and wife to live with them, to give them his grace, and to help them fulfill their rights and duties to God, to each other, and to their children faithfully until death.

(2) St. Paul tells us that marriage is a sign of union of Jesus and his Church. "Husbands, love your wives, as Christ loved the Church. He gave himself up for her to make her holy. . . . This is a great foreshadowing; I mean that it refers to Christ and the Church" (Eph 5, 25. 32). He describes the Church as the bride of Christ, made beautiful by her spouse. Jesus offered his life for his bride to make her holy.

(3) The sacrament gives sanctifying grace, the divine life, and all the actual graces needed throughout married life to bring about an ever deeper union of man and wife in soul and body so that they may live up to what they promised in their marriage vows and in their vocation of parenthood.

113. Why was marriage instituted?

Marriage was instituted (1) to bring children into the world and to educate them, (2) and also for the love of the spouses for each other.

(1) From married love come children. In his love for us God gives us life and the care we need as children from parents.

(2) From marriage a man and his wife have a loving companionship that is stronger than any other in life. The Lord God said: "That is why a man leaves his father and mother and clings to his wife, and the two of them become one body" (Gn 2, 24).

114. How long does the bond of marriage last?

The bond of marriage lasts until the death of one of the spouses; therefore, divorce is an evil.

Marriage is for life. It lasts as long as both parties live. Marriage is permanent because Jesus taught that married people should belong completely to each other just as he belongs completely to his Church. Jesus forbade divorce and remarriage. He said, "Let no man separate what God has joined" (Mk 10, 9).

115. What is the calling of every family?

The calling of every family is to share life together with a deep, personal love according to God's will.

It is the family's calling to become a community, sharing life together in deep love. The family is the most sacred of all societies. Our character, beliefs, thoughts, and virtues come from good loving parents.

116. What is the aim of family life?

Family life has this aim: that the spouses be ready with generous hearts to work together with the love of the Creator who through them will enlarge and enrich his own family day by day.

Marriage is a lifelong partnership of love. The giving of self in marriage brings children who make the love of husbands and wives richer and fulfills one of the purposes of marriage. If husbands and wives are generous to God in working with him according to his will, enlarging his own family on earth, he will bless them in this life and especially in heaven.

Catechesis for a Worshiping Community, no. 130

A. FILL IN THE BLANKS

1. Marriage was instituted by .... and given by him certain .... (109)

2. Marriage of the baptized was raised to the dignity of a sacrament by .... (110)

3. The ministers of the sacrament of matrimony are .... (111)

4. The dignity of the sacrament of matrimony shows itself in this: that the spouse (1) live together ....; (2) imitate Christ's own love for ....; (3) are consecrated to .... and to .... (112)

5. Marriage was instituted (1) to .... (2) and also for .... (113)

6. The bond of marriage lasts until .... (114)

7. The calling of every family is to .... (115)

8. Family life has this aim: that the spouses be ready with a generous heart to .... (116)

B. BIBLE READING   John 2, 1-11

The Marriage at Cana

Jesus went with his disciples to a town in Galilee called Cana, to be present at a wedding. The mother of Jesus was at this wedding as a friend of the family, for Nazareth, where she lived, was near Cana. Before the wedding feast was over, all the wine had been used. Mary understood how badly these people felt. The mother of Jesus believed that her Son had the power to do whatever he wished, and she said to him, "They have no wine."

Jesus said to her, "What would you have me do? My hour has not yet come."

It was not yet time for so public a miracle. However, at the request of his mother, Jesus was willing to help.

But since his mother knew that Jesus would in some way help the people in their need, she said to the servants who were waiting at the table, "Do whatever he tells you."

In the dining hall were standing six large stone jars, each about as large as a barrel, holding twenty-five gallons. These jars hold water for washing. Jesus said to the servants, "Fill the jars with water."

The servants obeyed Jesus and filled the jars up to the brim. Then Jesus spoke to them again and said, "Now pour out what you need from the jars and take it to the chief steward of the feast."

They drew out from the jars some of the water, which they had poured into them, and saw that it had been turned into wine. As the chief steward did not know where the servants had gotten the wine, he said to the young man who had just been married, "At a feast everybody gives the best wine first, and later he brings on wine that is not so good; but you have kept the good wine until now.'

Mary said to Jesus, "They have no wine."

This was the first time that Jesus used the power that God had given him, to do what no other man could do. When the disciples saw this miracle, they believed in Jesus more fully than before.

Discussion:

1. What did the mother of Jesus do when she saw that the wine had been used up?
2. How many stone jars were there and how much did each jar hold?
3. What did Jesus tell the servants to do?
4. What happened to the water in the jars?
5. Does this miracle teach us how great is the power of Mary's prayers?
6 What does this miracle have to do with marriage?

C. PRACTICE

1. The graces of the sacrament of marriage are given to be used in the daily life of a Christian husband, wife and family. Parents and children should use the sacraments of penance and Holy Eucharist often, and they should use them with their state of life in mind, seeking by means of confession to rid themselves of the faults which prevent a happy family life, and by means of Holy Communion to grow in love for one another in Christ.
2. Children should pray for their parents, brothers and sisters that they may share life together with a sincere personal love according to God's will. They should do all they can to bring this about by love, respect, patience, and obedience.

JESUS SPEAKS:

"I assure you, unless you change and become like little children, you will not enter the kingdom of God. Whoever makes himself lowly, becoming like this child, is of greatest importance in that heavenly reign."   (Mt 18, 3, 4)

Jesus died to take away our Sins

Part Seven — SIN

CHAPTER

18 The Sins of Human Beings

117. **What is man's greatest problem in working out his salvation?**

In working out his salvation, man's greatest problem is sin.

Working out our salvation means doing God's will. The sinner wants to live without regard for God's will. He chooses whatever he thinks will make him happy even though it does not fit into God's plan for him. He does not trust God's love for him.

118. **How was original sin committed?**

(1) God made man in a state of holiness, but man abused his liberty at the urging of the Evil One. (2) He set himself against God and looked for happiness apart from God.

(1) Man was the crown of God's creation; of all on earth he alone could give back to God the love which God first gave him. God wanted men to live as his family, united to each other and to himself in love. Nothing was to disturb this family: sickness, death, ignorance, weakness.

119

(2) But Adam abused his liberty. He disobeyed and rejected God's care. He wanted to search for happiness in his own way.

119. How is man born in original sin?

Man is born in original sin because fallen human nature, stripped of the grace that clothed it, hurt in its natural powers, and subjected to death, was carried on to all men.

When Adam sinned, he cut himself off from God. He was stripped of the grace God had given him. His human nature was harmed in its natural powers. Sickness and death entered his life. Adam's descendants were to suffer in the same way. Men are born into this world separated from their loving Father and subject to death. The main sign of sin in the world is man rejecting God. Other signs are war, poverty, hunger, hatred of people, violence, and other injustices.

120. What is personal sin?

Personal sin is committed by a person who, acting knowingly and willingly, breaks the moral law.

Sin is willful disobedience to God. This disobedience may be an action, a thought, a desire or an intention.

121. What happens when the sinner commits a personal sin?

The sinner who commits a personal sin (1) fails in love of God, (2) turns away from his goal of doing God's will, (3) and by serious offense (mortal sin), breaks his relationship with the Father.

(1) The sinner fails in love of God because he is willing to turn against God.

(2) The sinner chooses to do his own will rather than God's will. He is willing to displease God and even lose his friendship.

(3) Serious or mortal sin is a rejection of God which destroys the life shared between God and the sinner. It is a serious violation of the law of God.

A small violation of the law of God (venial sin) does not take away God's life from the soul or break God's friendship, but it weakens our love for God and harms ourselves and others.

The effect of mortal sin is separation from God and damage to ourselves and others. If we do not wish to change and continue to refuse to do what God wants us to do, the separation from God lasts. The Church calls this permanent separation from God "hell."

122. What must the Christian have to commit a sin?

To commit a sin the Christian must have (1) clear knowledge of right and wrong, (2) so as to be able to choose with an informed conscience to love God and avoid offending him.

(1) The person who commits the sin must know what he is doing and that what he is doing is an offense against God.

(2) There must be full consent of the will in the case of a serious sin.

123. What must we believe concerning God's forgiveness?

We must believe (1) that God is merciful and will pardon the sinner who is truly sorry (2) and by the power of his grace will draw him to salvation.

(1) Only God can forgive our sins. He chose his Son to be the one to suffer and to die for our sins. Jesus is called our Savior because he saved us from sin. God will pardon us if we are truly sorry for our sins and want to change our sinful ways. We can always look to God for merciful forgiveness.

(2) In the sacrament of penance Jesus forgives our sins, and gives us the peace which belongs to God's children. He also gives

us his grace to overcome sin in the future. He gives us the strength to be faithful to God's law of love. Through his grace he draws us to salvation.

Teacher reference: Principal Elements, no. 98

A. FILL IN THE BLANKS

1. In working out his salvation man's greatest problem is .... (117)

2. (1) Original sin was committed because man abused his .... at the urging of .... (2) He set himself against .... and looked for happiness apart from .... (118)

3. Man is born in original sin because fallen human nature, stripped of ...., hurt in ...., and subjected to ...., was carried on to .... (119)

4. Personal sin is committed by a person who .... (120)

5. A sinner who commits a personal sin (1) fails in ...., (2) turns away from ...., (3) and by serious offense breaks .... (121)

6. To commit a sin the Christian must have (1) ...., (2) so as to be able to .... to love God and avoid offending him. (122)

7. We must believe (1) that God is merciful and will .... (2) and by the power of his grace will .... (123)

B. BIBLE READING   Luke 15, 11-32

The Prodigal Son

There was a man who had two sons. The younger one said to his father, "Father, give me my share of the property." And when the father had given him his share, the young man went to a distant country and spent the money foolishly.

And when he had spent all he had, there was a severe famine in that country, and he became hungry. So he got a job as a keeper of pigs. For food he had to be satisfied with what was left over after the pigs had finished eating.

When he came to his right mind, he said to himself, "How many of my father's servants have enough to eat and to spare, and here I am dying of hunger. I will go back to my father, and say to him, 'Father, I have sinned against heaven and against you, and

am no longer worthy to be called your son. Let me be a hired servant in your house.' "

So he started homeward. But while he was still a long way off, the father saw him. He ran to meet him, and kissed him and held him tightly. "Father, I have done wrong in the sight of God, and of you!" cried the boy; "I am not worthy to be called your son."

But the father said to his servants, "Bring out the best clothes and put them on him, and put a ring on his finger, and shoes on his feet, and let us feast and be glad today, for this son of mine was dead and is alive again. He was lost and is found!" And they had a great feast.

But the elder son had been out in the field all the while, and now he came near to the house.

"How many years have I obeyed you," said the elder son to his father, "and you never even gave a young goat to eat with my friends. But now that this rascal comes back after wasting all your money, you give a grand feast for him!"

"Son," said his father, "you are always with me, and all that I have is yours. Let us be happy and rejoice, for your brother was dead, and has come to life; he was lost, and is found."

Discussion:

1. What did the younger son ask his father to do for him?
2. What happened to the younger son after he left his father?
3. What happened when the younger brother came home?
4. What did the father tell the servants to do?
5. What did the older son say to his father?
6. What answer did the father give his older son?
7. What does this story teach us about the sacrament of penance?

C. PRACTICE

1. Since mortal sin is treated so lightly by the world, we must always strive to keep alive in ourselves a real hatred of it. We can do this by remembering the sufferings and death of Jesus Christ, the price for the mortal sins of men.

2. In order to avoid mortal sin we must try to avoid even less serious sins. If we are faithful to God in smaller things we shall be faithful to him in serious things. We should pray for help from God when we are tempted to sin. If we do so, God will always give us strength to overcome temptation. In order to avoid sin we must also avoid any person, place or thing which may lead us into sin.

JESUS SPEAKS:

"If a man wishes to come after me, he must deny his very self, take up his cross, and begin to follow in my footsteps."

(Mt 16, 24)

"Pray that you may not be put to the test."   (Lk 22, 40)

"What profit would a man show if he were to gain the whole world and destroy himself in the process? What can a man offer in exchange for his very self?"

(Mt 16, 26)

The Grace of Jesus makes us holy

Part Eight — THE LIFE OF GRACE

CHAPTER

19 The New Life in the Spirit

124. **What happens when a man accepts the Spirit of Christ?**

When man accepts the Spirit of Christ, God leads him to a new way of life.

All Persons of the Blessed Trinity have a part in the holy work of getting and giving grace to people. The work of giving grace is especially the work of the Holy Spirit because it is a work of love, and the Holy Spirit is the Spirit of Love of the Father and the Son. He makes souls holy through the gift of grace.

125. **What does this new way of life do for man?**

This new way of life gives a man the power (1) to share in God's own life, (2) and to be joined to the Father and to Christ in a union of love which not even death can break.

(1) The Spirit brings God's life to man and all that he does so that a person is said to live in the "state of grace." Grace is God's gift of himself from which comes our life in God which is the life of grace.

This new life gives us the power to share in God's own life by the virtues of faith, hope, and love. Faith is a free gift by which the Holy Spirit helps us to accept God's word and to realize that God loves us and cares for us and that we can count on him. We can hope because in Jesus Christ God has promised us his love and care forever and will never leave us if only we remain united with him. Charity is the love of God and of our fellow men because they too belong to God. The presence in us of the Holy Spirit means we are able to love with the love of God, even our enemies, if we want to do so.

(2) Grace is God's gift of himself. By grace we are united to the Father and to Christ in a union of love. Jesus said, "Anyone who loves me will be true to my word, and my Father will love him; we will come to him and make our dwelling place with him" (Jn 14, 23).

126. What does the indwelling Holy Spirit give a man?

The indwelling Holy Spirit (1) gives a man hope and courage, (2) heals his weakness of soul, (3) helps him overcome his evil desires and selfishness (4) and practice virtues such as love and patience, (5) and makes his prayer more pleasing to God.

(1) Through sanctifying grace, and the powers of faith, hope, and love that come with it, and through actual grace (the help we need for mind and will to be good), we are made holy by the Holy Spirit who lives in our soul. His presence gives us the hope that God will grant us the help we need to save our soul and live with God forever in heaven; at the same time his presence gives us the courage and strength we need to accept the suffering and troubles of life.

(2) The Holy Spirit gives us actual grace, that special help which gives light to our mind and strength to our will to do good and to avoid evil.

(3) Evil persons, places, and things in this world can lead us into sin. The desires of our body also tempt us to do things un-

worthy of a Christian such as impurity, laziness, gluttony, anger, envy, pride, and neglect of our neighbor's needs. We need the help of the Holy Spirit to lead a good Christian life.

(4) Only when we allow the Holy Spirit to guide us and when we use the help of his grace can we continue to share in God's divine life of grace and live as his children.

(5) The Holy Spirit unites us with God by love and helps us to keep our friendship with him by prayer. He makes our prayer more pleasing to God because through the grace of the Holy Spirit our life too is pleasing to God.

127. What is sanctifying grace?

Sanctifying grace is a gift of God that makes us holy and pleasing to him.

By sanctifying grace our soul shares in the very life of God even while on this earth. Grace makes us holy and pleasing to God because it helps us to live as God's obedient children.

128. What does grace do for us?

Through grace the Holy Spirit helps us (1) to die to sin, (2) to share in the divinity of the Son of God by helping us live as children of God, (3) and to be closely united with the Most Holy Trinity by love.

(1) With the help of the grace of the Holy Spirit we are able to die to sin and live to God. We receive the strength we need to sacrifice ourselves by avoiding everything that would lead us into sin. With his help we can overcome our desires to do whatever might be against God's commandments.

(2) By grace we share in the divine life of the Son of God because we are adopted children of God. We became God's children in baptism when for the first time we received a new life of grace.

(3) St. Paul reminds Christians that they are the temple of God. "Are you not aware that you are the temple of God, and that the Spirit of God dwells in you?" (1 Cor 3, 16). The Holy Spirit was sent in order that he might make the Church holy. Through him the Father gives life to men who are willing to give up sin, because he is the Spirit of life. United in Jesus as his followers, we are led by the Holy Spirit in our journey to the kingdom of our heavenly Father. He helps us to fulfill our duties. He prompts us to strive for what is good. He encourages us to pray. His grace unites us to the Most Holy Trinity by love.

129. What has God willed for our salvation?

God has willed (1) that we receive the sanctifying grace of adoption as God's children (2) and gain eternal life.

(1) Our greatest honor is to be children of God. St. Paul says, "All who are led by the Spirit of God are sons of God" (Rom 8, 14). Grace is God's gift to us. We could never have earned it. Jesus bought grace for all men by his suffering and death and resurrection. Man had no right to grace.

(2) Through grace we also can gain eternal life. Through the merits of the death and resurrection of Jesus we hope to be united with God forever.

130. What is man's greatest dignity?

Man's greatest dignity is to have supernatural life because of the grace of Christ the Savior.

We received two lives from God. One is the natural life we received at birth. The other is the second we received when we were baptized Christians. Jesus said to Nicodemus, "I solemnly assure you, no one can see the reign of God unless he is begotten from above" (Jn 3, 3). We obtain natural life from our father and mother; we obtain supernatural life from God our Father. St. John says, "See what love the Father has bestowed on us in letting us be called children of God! Yet that is what we are" (1 Jn 3, 1).

Our greatest honor is to be children of God and to have God's life in our soul because of the grace of Christ the Savior. We must try to live a holy life and train ourselves to keep God's grace as our most precious treasure. We must ask the Holy Spirit to help us live according to our great dignity as children of God and as true Christians.

Teacher reference: Principal Elements, no. 98

A. FILL IN THE BLANKS

1. When man accepts the Spirit of Christ, God leads him to .... (124)
2. This new way of life gives man the power (1) to .... (2) and to be joined to .... in a union of .... (125)
3. The indwelling Holy Spirit (1) gives a man ...., (2) heals ...., (3) helps him overcome ...., (4) and practice virtues such as ...., (5) and .... more pleasing to God. (126)
4. Sanctifying grace is .... that makes us .... (127)
5. Through grace the Holy Spirit helps us (1) to die to .... to share in .... by helping us to .... (128)
6. God has willed that we receive (1) .... (2) and gain .... (129)
7. Man's great dignity is .... because of .... (130)

B. BIBLE READING   John 3, 1-21

Nicodemus

Among those who listened to Jesus was a man named Nicodemus. He was a ruler of the Jews, a Pharisee. The Pharisees were men who kept all the laws of Moses very strictly; and they kept many other rules besides, which they themselves had made. They were proud of their strictness, and thought themselves better than other people, even better than Jesus. They would not listen to Jesus.

But Nicodemus was not like the other Pharisees. He heard Jesus teach, and saw the miracles, and he wondered what kind of man this Jesus might be. Nicodemus did not quite dare to speak to Jesus openly, for fear the other Pharisees would laugh at him.

Jesus talks to Nicodemus

But he did want to know more about this teacher who talked so much about God and the kingdom of God.

So Nicodemus went to Jesus one night. He said to Jesus, "Teacher, we know that God sent you, for no one can do these miracles that you do unless God were with him."

Jesus said to him, "No one can see the kingdom of God unless he is born again."

Nicodemus did not understand. Surely, he would like to see the kingdom of God. But he was a grown man. Must he be born again?

Jesus said, "No one can enter into God's kingdom without being begotten of water and the Spirit."

Then Jesus went on to explain. "Do not be surprised that I tell you you must all be begotten from above. The wind blows where it will. You hear the sound it makes but you don't know where it comes from, or where it goes. So it is with everyone begotten of the Spirit."

Jesus meant to say that if we believe in him, the Holy Spirit gives us a new life. We are "born again." We become children of God. We cannot understand how the Holy Spirit gives us this new life, just as we cannot understand how the wind blows.

But Jesus said to Nicodemus, "Yes, God so loved the world that he gave his only Son, so that whoever believes in him may not die but mav have eternal life."

Nicodemus was a good man. He kept the law of God carefully. But that was not enough to open the way into the kingdom of God. Unless the Holy Spirit gives us a new life, we cannot see the kingdom of God. We call this life sanctifying grace, which is God's life in us. We receive this grace for the first time in baptism.

Nicodemus listened carefully. He had never heard such wonderful words. He could not understand. But when he went away he thought about it. And after a while he did believe in Jesus. He was born again, and he became a child of God.

Discussion:

1. Who was Nicodemus?
2. Why did Nicodemus come to Jesus?
3. What did Jesus tell Nicodemus?
4. Did Nicodemus believe in Jesus?
5. How do the words of Jesus explain the grace of God and the Holy Spirit?
6. Why do the words of Jesus refer to baptism?

C. PRACTICE

1. Since grace, which is a share in the life of God, is a free gift from God to which we have no right, we should show that it means very much to us. We do this by avoiding everything that may be sinful, for this may put us in danger of losing God's grace. We should make frequent use of the sacraments of penance and Holy Communion, through which we can grow in God's grace. We should pray often, for prayer helps us to continue in this life of God and brings us many actual graces, or help from God, which are light for our mind and strength for our will.

I am the Way, the Truth and the Life

Part Nine — THE MORAL LIFE

CHAPTER
20

Human and Christian Freedom

131. **What is God's plan concerning freedom?**

God's plan is that man, united with Jesus Christ, should give a free answer to God's call.

It is part of man's dignity and duty to be free, since he is responsible for his actions. He must keep the law of God which is taught by Jesus. He must be free to answer God's call. He can do so with the help of Jesus Christ.

132. **How was freedom harmed?**

At the beginning, God gave the gift of freedom to human nature, but this has been badly harmed by original sin, the sin of humanity.

God gave his grace to Adam and Eve. It was the greatest of his gifts to them because they shared in the very life of God. They were truly free with the freedom of children of God. But through sin the human race lost God's life, grace. Even our freedom was badly harmed by original sin, the sin of humanity.

133. How is human weakness overcome?

Human weakness after original sin is overcome by grace, so that man can live with holiness in the faith of Jesus Christ.

Our hope lies in the grace of Jesus Christ, merited for us by his death on the cross. The freedom of fallen man has been so weakened that he would be unable for long to fulfill his duties to God and his neighbor without the help of God's grace. Our freedom is so raised and strengthened that we can live a life pleasing to God in the faith of Jesus Christ.

134. Why does the Church promote human freedom?

The Church promotes human freedom (1) for man's welfare on earth (2) and for the higher good of grace and eternal salvation.

(1) The Church tries to promote true freedom for the good of mankind on earth, defends freedom against unjust force, and asks Christians to work together to protect freedom.

(2) But the Church especially defends freedom for the spiritual welfare of mankind. The Church claims that man's answer to God in faith must be free. No one is to be forced to accept the Christian faith against his own will. The Church claims freedom for itself as a society of men who have the right to live according to the Christian faith, which leads to man's welfare on earth and eternal salvation in heaven.

Teacher reference: Principal Elements, no. 101

A. FILL IN THE BLANKS

1. God's plan concerning freedom is that man, united with Jesus Christ, ... (131)
2. God's gift of freedom to human nature at the beginning has been badly harmed by ...., the sin of .... (132)
3. Human weakness after original sin is overcome by ...., so that man can .... (133)
4. The Church promotes human freedom (1) for .... (2) and for .... (134)

B. BIBLE READING

John 15, 5-8

The Vine and the Branches

After the Passover supper, Jesus said many things to comfort his beloved disciples before he left them. He had just given them the Eucharist, for he changed the bread and wine into his body and blood. He told them to offer the Mass in memory of him, having given them the power to consecrate the bread and wine as he did. To show how closely he would be united with them through the Eucharist he said,

"I am the vine, you are the branches. He who lives in me and I in him, will produce abundantly, for apart from me you can do nothing. A man who does not live in me is like a withered, rejected branch, picked up to be thrown in the fire and burnt.

"If you live in me, and my words stay part of you, you may ask what you will—it will be done for you. My Father has been glorified in your bearing much fruit and becoming my disciples."

It is God's plan that, united with Jesus, we willingly do God's will. By the grace of Jesus we can overcome our human weakness. The grace of God is like the sap that goes through the vine into the branches to give them life and strength. Jesus is the vine, and we are the branches.

Discussion:

1. When did Jesus speak these words?
2. Who is the vine and who are the branches?
3. What will happen if we are united with Jesus, the vine?
4. What will happen if we do not remain united with Jesus?
5. What does Jesus promise through our prayers if we remain with him?
6. Can we overcome our human weaknesses without the grace of Christ?

C. PRACTICE

1. God is always offering us actual graces, that is, the help we need to do good and to avoid evil. He gives us light for our minds and strength for our wills. Each day we should pray that we may make good use of his graces. God sends us these graces in order that we may do good deeds which will make God's life grow in our souls. Since we are free to accept or refuse these graces, we should pray that we may use God's graces well and in this way answer his call.
2. The Holy Spirit, who dwells in our soul as in a temple, is the giver of light and strength. We should often pray for him that he may change us as he changed the apostles on Pentecost. We shall then be true witnesses of Jesus Christ.

God wants us to know, love and serve Him

CHAPTER

21

The Moral Life of Christians

135. **If we are to answer God's love, what must we do?**

If we are to answer God's love we must (1) observe everything that Christ has commanded, (2) and believe all that he has taught.

(1) The teaching of the Church includes all those things which are to be done or avoided in order that the followers of Jesus might live the Christian life according to his will. If we truly love God we shall try to do his holy will in everything.

(2) The teaching of the Church includes all the truths of faith which Jesus taught. Before ascending into heaven Jesus said, "Teach them to carry out everything I have commanded you" (Mt 28, 20).

136. **What does Christian morality teach?**

Christian morality teaches us a way of living a life worthy of a human being and of an adopted son of God, that we may grow in the new life given to us through Jesus Christ.

Christian morality shows us a way of life worthy of a human being and a child of God, that we may grow in the grace and love of God. The Church expresses its teaching by stating ideals, by making judgments about the morality of certain actions, and by making laws concerning human behavior.

137. How is Christian morality supported and guided?

Christian morality is supported and guided by the grace and gifts of the Holy Spirit.

So that we may live well as God's children, the Holy Spirit helps us to respect each other because united in Christ we share his life of grace. He gives us the desire and the help we need to do things pleasing to our heavenly Father. He makes clear what Jesus taught us in the gospel, and helps us to remain true to Jesus and to his Church. These helps of the Holy Spirit may be called actual graces. Without these helps it is impossible to do anything toward our own salvation or the salvation of others.

138. What is conscience?

Conscience is a personal judgment that something is right or wrong because of the Will and law of God.

Our conscience is our mind judging on moral matters. Our conscience tells us whether an action is right or wrong, a mortal or a venial sin. It helps us to know when we act sinfully. Conscience must be instructed according to the teaching of Christ and his Church.

139. Must each person have a right conscience?

Each person must have a right conscience and follow it.

The moral life of Christians must be guided by the grace and gifts of the Holy Spirit. We must have a gift conscience and follow it.

140. **How must a Catholic form a right conscience?**
A Catholic must form a right conscience by obeying the teaching authority of God's Church.

We do not always know whether our conscience is right. But we can train our conscience by listening to the Word of God in the gospels and in the Church and by being attentive to the inspiration of the Holy Spirit within us.

141. **What does obedience to the Holy Spirit include?**
Obedience to the Holy Spirit includes a faithful observance of (1) the commandments of God, (2) the laws of the Church, (3) and just civil laws.

We should let the Holy Spirit have his way with us. He will bend our wills and touch our hearts if we will let him. We ought to pray each day for the strength to say yes to what the Spirit wants to do in us. Obedience to him includes a faithful observance of (1) the commandments of God, (2) the laws of the Church, (3) and just civil laws.

Teacher reference: Principal Elements, no. 103

A. FILL IN THE BLANKS

1. If we are to answer God's love we must (1) ....
   (2) and .... (135)
2. Christian morality teaches us .... worthy
   of .... and of ...., that we may grow in
   .... given to us through .... (136)
3. Christian morality is supported and guided by .... (137)
4. Conscience is .... that something is ....
   because of .... (138)
5. Each person must have a .... conscience and .... it. (139)
6. A Catholic forms a right conscience by .... (140)
7. Obedience to the Holy Spirit includes a faithful observance
   of (1) ...., (2) the laws of ...., (3) and .... (141)

B. BIBLE READING   Matthew 28, 16-20

The Last Instruction of Jesus

Forty days after the Resurrection, the followers of Jesus met on a mountain in Galilee. More than five hundred people were gathered at this time; and there Jesus showed himself to them all. He said to his apostles, "Full authority has been given to me both in heaven and on earth; go, therefore, and make disciples of all the nations. Baptize them in the name 'of the Father, and of the Son, and of the Holy Spirit.' Teach them to carry out everything I have commanded you. And know that I am with you always, until the end of the world!"

Then Jesus led them out near Bethany, and with hands upraised, blessed them. As he blessed, he left them, and was taken up to heaven. They fell down to do him reverence, then returned to Jerusalem filled with joy. There they were to be found in the temple constantly, speaking the praises of God.

"You are to be My witnesses even to the ends of the earth."

Discussion:

1. Where did Jesus meet his followers on this occasion?
2. What did Jesus say to his apostles?
3. When he told them to carry out everything he had commanded them, what did he mean?
4. What did Jesus mean when he said that he would be with them always?
5. What did Jesus do after he gave his last instructions?
6. What did the Apostles do after Jesus was taken up to heaven?

C. PRACTICE

1. The kind of happiness which Jesus Christ promises in this life comes from loving God and being loved by God, and from the hope of eternal happiness in heaven. Jesus did not promise us pleasure or wealth. But he tells us that it is only through suffering and self-sacrifice that we can have joy and peace of soul in this life. He has not only told us how to live, but has shown us by his example. What is more, he gives us all the help we need to follow his example. We should, therefore, learn to know and love Jesus Christ. We can do so by frequently reading the gospels and studying the teaching of the Church about what we must believe and how we must observe what Jesus has commanded.

2. If we love Christ and try to follow his example we shall receive the strength he promised especially in the sacrament of the Eucharist and in prayer.

JESUS SPEAKS:

"I give you a new commandment: Love one another. Such as my love has been for you, so must your love be for each other. This is how all will know you are my disciples: your love for one another."   (Jn 13, 34. 35)

"The command I give you is this, that you love one another."

(Jn 15, 17)

Holiness means being in love with God

22 Perfect Christian Love

142. In what are all commandments summed up?

All commandments are summed up in faith working through love.

The moral teaching of Jesus is summed up in the two commandments he gave his Church: "You shall love the Lord your God with all your heart, with all your soul, with all your mind, and with all your strength. . . . You shall love your neighbor as yourself" (Mk 12, 29-31). Other words and the example of Jesus tell of how these commandments are to practiced.

143. What is man's greatest responsibility?

Man's greatest responsibility is to do God's Will (1) by keeping his commandments and living in his love, (2) and by practicing the "new commandment" of love of neighbor.

(1) Jesus said, "As the Father has loved me, so I have loved you. Live on in my love. You will live in my love if you keep my commandments, even as I have kept my Father's commandments, and live in his love" (Jn 15, 9-10).

(2) One can tell the true Christian by the love he shows for his fellow man. Jesus said, "I give you a new commandment: love one another. Such as my love has been for you, so must your love be for each other. This is how all will know you for my disciples: your love for one another" (Jn 13, 34-35).

144. What is a man's holiness?

A man's holiness, whatever his state of life may be, is perfect love of God.

The life of Jesus shows us in a human way that God's life is a life of love. Father, Son, and Holy Spirit are forever giving themselves to each other.

God asks us to be holy. To be holy means being like God. This means sharing more and more of our life with him so that he can finish the good work he began in us through his grace in baptism when we first received his divine life and became his children. Jesus said, "You must be made perfect as your heavenly Father is perfect" (Mt 5, 48). Our holiness is perfect love of God.

145. Why is love of God the soul of morality?

Love of God is the soul of morality because God is love, and in God's plan that love reaches out in Jesus Christ, to unite men in their love for one another.

(1) God loves us. He always has loved us and always will love us. He watches over us every moment of our life. He gave us all the good things in life that we have, our life, our health, our family, our friends. God made us his children in baptism and promised to grant us eternal life with him in heaven, if we are faithful to him.

(2) God's love reaches us through Jesus. In his perfect love for us Jesus died on the cross to make up for our personal sins and regain for us the life of grace and eternal life with God. By means of his personal presence and the gift of sanctifying grace, the Holy Spirit makes men pleasing to God and holy. He makes us children in the family of God and unites us in faith and love to Christ and to each other. St. John says, "Beloved, let us love one another because love is of God; everyone who loves is begotten of God and has knowledge of God. The man without love has known nothing of God, for God is love" (1 Jn 4, 7-8).

146. Why do men and women accept a religious vocation?

Men and women accept a religious vocation to show in this special and needed way their love of God and true service to mankind.

The perfection of Christian life consists in love: first in the love of God, then in the love of neighbor. The whole life of a religious is to be one continuous act of love in the service of God and the Church. The religious state was begun by our Lord when he taught us to practice poverty, chastity, and obedience. Religious take these three vows of religion to help them live a life of love for God and neighbor.

Teacher reference: Principal Elements, no. 91

A. FILL IN THE BLANKS

1. All commandments are summed up in .... (142)

2. Man's greatest responsibility is .... (1) by...............
   (2) and by .... (143)

3. Man's holiness is .... (144)

4. Love of God is the soul of morality because ....,
   and in God's plan that love reaches out in ....,
   to unite men in .... (145)

5. Men and women accept a religious vocation to .... (146)

B. BIBLE READING   Luke 10, 25-38

The Good Samaritan

At that time one of the Scribes—men who wrote copies of the books of the Old Testament, studied them, and taught them— came to Jesus and asked him a question, "Teacher, what must I do to inherit everlasting life?"

Jesus answered him, "What is written in the law?"

The Scribe said, "You shall love the Lord your God with all your heart, with all your soul, with all your strength, and with all your mind; and your neighbor as yourself."

Jesus said to him, "You have answered correctly. Do this and you shall live."

The Good Samaritan

But the man was not satisfied. He asked another question, "And who is my neighbor?"

To answer this question, Jesus told the story of a good Samaritan. He said, "There was a man going down from Jerusalem to Jericho who fell among robbers. They stripped him, beat him, and then went off leaving him half-dead. A priest happened to be going down the same road; he saw him but continued on. And a Levite also, when he came to the place and saw the man, he too went by on the other side. But a Samaritan who was going down, came where this man was; and as soon as he saw him, he felt pity for him.

"He came to the man and dressed his wounds, pouring oil and wine into them. Then he lifted him up, set him on his own beast and brought him to an inn. There he took care of him all night. The next morning he took out from his purse two coins and gave them to the keeper of the inn and said, 'Take care of him; and if you need to spend more than this, do so and when I come again, I will pay it to you.'

"Which one of these three do you think showed himself a neighbor to the man who fell among the robbers?"

The Scribe said, "The one who showed mercy to him."

Jesus said to him, "Then go and do the same."

Discussion:

1. What did the Scribe want to know?
2. How did the Scribe say what was written in the law?
3. What did the priest and the Levite do when they saw the man who fell among robbers?
4. What did the Samaritan do when he found the man who was robbed?
5. What did Jesus tell the Scribe to do?
6. How does this story explain perfect Christian love?

C. PRACTICE

1. We have been made children of God, for in baptism we have received a new life from Christ. We must therefore live a new life according to the dignity of a Christian. The Christian life is a life of love. We would not be able to love God or one another as children of God without a special gift from God, the gift of charity. This gift is one of the great powers which God gives us with the gift of the divine life: the power to believe God, the power to hope in him and the power to love him and to love our fellow men as children of God. These gifts, together with the gifts of the Holy Spirit and other helps which God gives us, help us to live according to the new life which is more as members of the Mystical Body of Christ. Our one aim in life should be to practice our faith in God through love. This means that we should love God above all things for his own sake and to love ourselves and all our brothers as children of God for God's sake.

2. We express love for our fellow men by treating all men with reverence which they deserve as children of God. We must treat every man as we would Christ himself. We must practice the works of mercy.

We must Love God
and each other

CHAPTER 23 — Duties Flowing from Love of God and Man

147. How do we know the duties flowing from love of God and man?

We know the duties flowing from love of God and man from (1) the Ten Commandments of God; (2) the Sermon on the Mount, especially the Beatitudes; (3) the spiritual and corporal works of mercy; (4) the virtues and seven capital sins; (5) the laws of the Church.

(1) The *Ten Commandments* constitute an important part of the message of salvation to Moses. Like the first People of God we Christians accept the commandments as a part of our agreement of faithfulness to God. By keeping the commandments we give ourselves to God in loving obedience. All the commandments are contained in the two commandments of love of God and neighbor.

(2) The *Beatitudes* express some of the high standards of Christ's kingdom and the reward promised for living according to them.

(3) Some of the most important *works of mercy* are to help convert the sinner, advise the doubtful, instruct the ignorant, comfort the sorrowful, bear wrongs patiently, pray for the living and

the dead, feed the hungry, clothe the poor, visit the sick, and bury the dead.

(4) The *virtues* that concern God (theological) are faith, hope, and love. Virtues that concern man (moral) are: prudence, justice, temperance, fortitude.

(5) The laws o fthe Church are some duties expected of Catholic Christians today.

148. What are our duties toward God?

(1) The Will of God must be put first in our lives. (2) We must act as children toward God our all-good and all-loving Father, and never try to live apart from him. (3) We must gladly give God true worship and prayer.

The Will of God must be put first in our life. We must love him as obedient children because he is our all-good, all-loving Father. We must worship him at Holy Mass and in our prayers.

149. How do we sin against the honor due to God?

Idolatry is to put someone or something in place of God; blasphemy is to dishonor God by our words.

(1) The *First Commandment* is: "I, the Lord, am your God. You shall not have other gods besides me." It binds us to adoration. It warns us against any action that would lead us away from the true adoration of the living God: neglect to learn the truths God has taught, or refusal to believe these truths; leaving God's Church; giving in to superstitious practices.

(2) The *Second Commandment* is: "You shall not take the name of the Lord, your God, in vain." We must have respect for God's name and everything connected with it. We honor God's name by invoking God in our prayers and Holy Mass.

(3) The *Third Commandment* is: "Remember to keep holy the sabbath day." We are obliged to attend Mass each Sunday (or

Saturday evening) and holyday of obligation. The Mass is the highest form of worship. Sunday is a weekly reminder of our Lord's Easter victory and of the joy which God's people share with Christ. By resting from our usual work, we find it easier to join with other Christians in making Sunday a day of thanks for the triumph of Jesus Christ.

150. What are our duties toward our fellow man?

Like Christ, (1) we must show our love for our fellow man by concern for his rights: (2) we must reach out to help others; (3) our thoughts and words concerning others must be ruled by the love we owe the children of God; (4) we must respect and obey all lawful authority in the home, in society, and in the Church.

(1) Immediately beside the great law of the kingdom of God, "You shall love the Lord your God with all your heart," there is the command: "And your neighbor as yourself" (Lk 10, 27). The commandment of love of neighbor found in the Old Testament is carried over into the new dispensation, where it is renewed. Jesus declared that this commandment of fraternal love is his favorite and his own commandment. "This is my commandment: love one another as I have loved you" (Jn 15, 12). This love is the sign by which his disciples will be clearly recognized.

Today we are challenged to live our life in such a way that we will bear witness to God by serving the needs of man. As Christians, we can serve our fellow man by personally taking care of his spiritual, physical, and social needs—his freedom, housing, food, health, right to work.

(2) We must bring our Christian faith into a way of life based on the spirit of the gospel. This is the Christian life. The Church urges us to serve God by serving our fellow man after the example of Jesus Christ. Christians must be servants because Jesus was. Such a life calls for sacrifice and earnest effort. The

Church wants us to have room in our hearts for all peoples so that we might labor with all men to build up human society. We do this by reaching out to help others. A life of service to others is the best way of letting people know that God is present in the world and that he loves all men.

(3) God commands us to think kindly. Jesus said, "If you want to avoid judgment, stop passing judgment" (Mt 7, 1). Kindness excludes evil and suspicious thoughts.

Our speech concerning others must also be ruled by love. The sin of uncharitable talk destroys unity within any family. It violates truth, justice, and love.

(4) The *Fourth Commandment* is: "Honor your father and your mother. Authority is the right, power, and duty to govern the members of a family, the members of the Church, or the citizens of a country. All authority comes from God. The authority of parents is from God. Even the authority of the government comes from God. We who are members of the Mystical Body of Christ are to imitate the reverence which he showed for those in authority. We are commanded especially to give our parents respect and love. As children, we owe them obedience.

151. How do we sin against our neighbor?

We sin against our neighbor (1) when we show little interest in helping him in his needs; (2) when we steal, damage another's good name or property, cheat, and fail to pay our debts; (3) when we show anger and hatred; (4) when we are immodest in behavior and dress.

(1) It is sinful to be so selfish as to show no interest in helping others. Jesus reminded us that what we do for others we do for him.

(2) The *Seventh Commandment* is: "You shall not steal." The *Tenth Commandment* is: "You shall not covet anything that belongs

to your neighbor." All the goods of this world came from a good God. Material goods that God gives us are not for ourselves alone, but also for our family and others in need. The Seventh and Tenth Commandments forbid us to take something that belongs to another against his wish. Stealing, damaging the property of another, not paying just debts, wasting the money or property of an employer and depriving our family of needed money by drinking or foolish spending are all sins against these two commandments.

The *Eighth Commandment* is: "You shall not bear false witness against your neighbor." A good name is the esteem with which a person is held by others. To harm a person's good name is a sin both when the unkind talk is based on truth (detraction), and when it is based on a lie (calumny). Revealing a person's hidden faults and gossiping about a person's known faults are ways of damaging a person's reputation. It is never permitted to tell a lie.

(3) The *Fifth Commandment* is: "You shall not kill." This commandment directs us to care for our body, mind, and soul and to care for the body and soul of our neighbor. We must practice self-discipline in the use of food, alcohol, tobacco and drugs. Christ's followers are to oppose whatever may destroy or abuse human life. This commandment also forbids unjust anger, which leads to hatred, revenge, fighting, and quarreling.

(4) The *Sixth Commandment* is: "You shall not commit adultery." The *Ninth Commandment* is: "You shall not covet your neighbor's wife." The sex passion, implanted in us by God as a sacred power, is something holy. It is something important in God's plan of creation and providence. The misuse of it is evil. The full use of the sexual passion is a right and privilege of those who are validly married.

Sins against these commandments are: adultery, fornication, self-abuse. Though it is impossible to keep all evil thoughts and desires from our minds, we can, at least, refuse to give them a welcome. Unwelcomed desires, no matter how wrong they seem, cannot defile our heart.

152. **What are our duties toward self?**

We must (1) be an example of Christian goodness; (2) be humble and patient with ourselves and others; (3) be simple in the use of the things of this world; (4) be pure in words and actions; (5) avoid pride, laziness, envy, and intemperance in food and drink.

(1) No one has ever spent himself for others as Jesus when he dwelt among us. In his life in the world the Christian should try to imitate the love of Jesus in such a way that others will want to copy it. By his example of kindness to others he can spread the faith that is in him.

(2) The true way to holiness is to love God and our neighbor for God's sake, and to sacrifice ourselves in order to fulfill the great commandment of love. Our patience in our shortcomings and those of others pleases God.

(3) By the example of their spirit of simplicity in using the things of this world Christians can bear witness to the teaching of Christ in this world that is so taken up with material things.

(4) To this world, where the body and sensuality count for so much, the true Christian life of decency in word and action proves that purity is possible and pleasing to God. It gives greater freedom to serve the needs of people.

(5) If we pray God will always give us strength to overcome temptation. In order to avoid sin we must also avoid any person, place, or thing which will lead us into sin. We should pray in particular for the grace to guard against the principal sources of sin (capital sins) such as: pride, sloth, envy, and lack of self-control in food and drink.

Teacher reference: Principal Elements, no. 105

A. FILL IN THE BLANKS

1. We know the duties flowing from love of God and man from
   (1) .... (2) .... (3) ....
   .... (4) .... (5) .... (147)

2. Our duties toward God are: (1) .... must be
   first in our lives. (2) We must act as .... our all-
   good and all-loving Father, and never try to ....
   (3) We must gladly give God .... (148)

3. Idolatry is to ....; blasphemy is to .... (149)

4. Our duties toward our fellow man are: (1) like Christ we will
   show our love for our fellow man by ....; (2) we
   reach out to ....; (3) our thoughts and words concerning others will be ruled by ....; (4) we will ....
   all lawful authority in the ...., in ...., and
   in .... (150)

5. We sin against neighbor (1) when we show little interest ....
   .... (2) when we steal, damage another's ....,
   cheat, and not pay ....; (3) when we show ....;
   (4) when we are immodest in .... (151)

6. Our duties toward self are: we must (1) be an example of
   ....; (2) be humble and patient with ....;
   (3) be simple in the use of ....; (4) be pure in ....;
   (5) avoid .... (152)

B. BIBLE READING   Exodus 20, 1-17. 32. 33. 34.
The Ten Commandments

Moses brought the people out from the camp to the foot of
Mount Sinai. On the morning of the third day there was thunder
and lightning. All the mountain shook and gave out smoke like a
furnace. A trumpet sounded loudly. God began to speak from the
cloud.

Then God called Moses up to the top of Mount Sinai and gave
him commandments written on tablets of stone. God said:

"I, the Lord am your God. You shall not have other gods besides me.

"You shall not take the name of the Lord, your God, in vain.

"Remember to keep holy the sabbath day.

"Honor your father and your mother.

"You shall not kill.

"You shall not commit adultery.

"You shall not steal.

"You shall not bear false witness against your neighbor.

"You shall not covet your neighbor's wife.

Moses destroys the stone tablets and the golden calf

"You shall not covet anything that belongs to your neighbor."

Moses was with the Lord forty days and forty nights. The people became tired waiting for him. They went to Aaron and said, "Make us gods to worship."

Then Aaron said, "Bring your gold ornaments to me." He melted the gold, and from the metal he shaped an image of a calf.

Moses prayed God to spare the people. When he came down the mountainside, and saw the golden calf, and the people singing and dancing around it, he was angry. He threw down the tablets of stone and broke them at the foot of the mountain. The gold calf he burned and ground into powder.

Again Moses went up Mount Sinai, to pray for the people. God told him to make two tablets of stone like the ones he had broken. Moses wrote the Ten Commandments on them.

Discussion:

1. What happened on Mount Sinai before God began to speak from the cloud?
2. What are the first three commandments of God which are about him?
3. What are the fourth to the tenth commandments which are about our neighbor?
4. How long was Moses with the Lord?
5. What did the people do while Moses was on the mountain?
6. What did Moses do when he returned from the mountain?
7. Why did Moses return to the mountain?
8. Must we keep these same commandments today?

C. PRACTICE

1. We cannot love someone we do not know. God has told us of himself in order that we might love him. Because we are God's children we know God more than those who do not have the gift of faith. But we can get more knowledge of our faith by reading and study. To study our religion faithfully is a sign of our love for God. It is also an important way of loving him even more. By loving and serving God we can lead others to know him better because our good example does more good than words. We displease God by not caring to know more about him. By our bad example, we may be keeping others from loving him more.

2. Chastity is a virtue that is important to man and woman. Sex is something good and holy. There is nothing evil about any part of the body, but the sexual power may be used only in marriage. It is a means of cooperating with God in bringing children into the world. Any misuse of sex outside of marriage

is sinful. Boys and girls in their teens who are in no position to think of marriage for several years, or who have no thought of marriage at all, put themselves in the danger of committing serious sins if they take part in steady company-keeping. The misuse of sex is something shameful because it is the misuse of something sacred. It is a sin against love, not only against the love of God, as is every sin, but also against the love of our neighbor because we are leading another person into sin and making it possible for that person to offend God. The virtue of modesty draws us to guard our senses of sight, touch, and hearing, so as not to invite temptation. Modesty also helps us to be careful in our dress and behavior, so as not to cause temptation to others.

JESUS SPEAKS:

"You shall love the Lord your God with all your heart, with all your soul, with all your strength, and with all your mind; and your neighbor as yourself." (Lk 10, 27)

"He who obeys the commandments he has from me is the man who loves me; and he who loves me will be loved by my Father. I too will love him and reveal myself to him." (Jn 14, 21)

"You will live in my love if you keep my commandments, even as I have kept my Father's commandments, and live in his love." (Jn 15, 10)

"Anyone who loves me will be true to my word, and my Father will love him; we will come to him and make our dwelling place with him." (Jn 14, 23)

Mary, our Mother, leads us to Jesus

Part Ten — MARY AND THE SAINTS

CHAPTER
24

Mary Mother of God, Mother and Model of the Church

153. **Why is Mary in the Church in a place highest after Christ?**

Mary is in the Church in a place highest after Christ (1) because she is the ever-virgin Mother of Jesus Christ our Lord and God, (2) and because she is very close to us as our spiritual Mother.

(1) Mary is in the Church in a place highest after Christ because she is the Mother of God. An angel had come to ask her consent to God's wish that she should become the Mother of his Son. She not only consented, she also willed to be his Mother and to have an important part in his mission of saving the world.

(2) At the Incarnation at Nazareth, Mary gave Jesus to us. On Calvary, Jesus gave us his Mother. In becoming the Mother of God she also willed to become our spiritual Mother. Through her prayers to her Son we hope to reach salvation.

154. **What are some the special gifts Mary received from God?**

Some of the special gifts Mary received from God are: (1) being Mother of God, (2) being preserved from all stain of original sin, (3) being taken body and soul to heaven.

(1) The Blessed Virgin worked together with the Divine Word, the Son of God, and with the Holy Spirit in the great work of the Incarnation. She is the Mother of God, and this is the reason for all her power before God and for her holiness.

(2) In view of the merits of her Divine Son, Mary alone enjoyed the privilege of being preserved from original sin. Mary was never subject to the evil spirit. She was always in the state of sanctifying grace.

(3) After a most blessed death Mary was assumed into heaven with soul and body and was crowned Queen of Heaven by her own Son.

155. **What veneration do we owe to Mary?**

We owe special veneration by word and example to Mary as Mother of Christ, Mother of the Church, and our spiritual Mother.

The Church urges us to give special veneration to Mary as the Mother of God, the Mother of the Church, and our spiritual Mother. In doing this we imitate her Son who loved and honored his Mother more than any other human being. He made her holier and more beautiful than any other member of his Church, for she is truly the Mother of the Church. By following her example and by seeking her help in prayer we can be sure of reaching her Son in eternal life.

156. **Why does the Church honor the other saints?**

The Church honors the other saints who are already with the Lord in heaven (1) because they inspire us by the good example of their lives, (2) and because we ask them to pray to God for us.

(1) Because of our union with Christ we are united with all those who share his life in the larger family of God, the Communion of Saints. We honor the saints when we try to imitate the example of their virtuous lives.

(2) We honor them also when we pray to them. We on earth (Church Militant) are helped by the prayers of the victorious and blessed members of the family in heaven (Church Triumphant). We also share in their merits gained by their holy life.

157. **What is our duty toward the deceased?**

(1) We must have reverence toward the bodies of those who have gone before us in death, (2) and we must pray for deceased relatives, friends, and all the faithful departed.

(1) We show respect for the bodies of the deceased because they were temples of the Holy Spirit and are destined to rise gloriously.

(2) We can help the suffering members of God's family (Church Suffering) whose souls are being purified in purgatory. They can and do pray for us, even though they cannot help themselves. Through the Communion of Saints we are one with those loved ones and friends who rest in Christ.

Teacher reference: Principal Elements, no. 106

A. FILL IN THE BLANKS

1. Mary is in the Church in a place highest after Christ (1) because .... (2) and because .... (153)
2. Some of the special gifts Mary received from God are: (1) being .... (2) being ...., (3) being .... (154)

3. We owe special veneration by word and example to Mary as
.........................., and .... (155)

4. The Church honors the other saints who are already with the
Lord in heaven (1) because .... (2) and
because .... (156)

5. We must (1) .... toward the bodies of those who
have gone before us in death, (2) and we must .... (157)

B. BIBLE READING Luke 1, 26-38

The Annunciation

The hour was at hand for which God had been preparing his
people. The world was looking for a Redeemer. The Jews prayed
that God would now keep the promise he made to Adam and Eve
and had repeated again and again through the prophets.

The angel Gabriel was sent from God to the town of Nazareth,
in that part of the land called Galilee. There the angel found a
young girl named Mary, who was soon to be married to Joseph,
a very good man who also lived in Nazareth. Though Joseph was
a carpenter, he was a relative of King David. The angel came
into the room where Mary was and said to her, "Rejoice, O highly
favored daughter! The Lord is with you. Blessed are you among
women."

Mary was surprised at the angel's words and wondered what they could mean. The angel spoke again and said, "Do not fear, Mary. You have found favor with God. You shall conceive and bear a son and give him the name Jesus. Great will be his dignity and he will be called Son of the Most High. The Lord God will give him the throne of David his father. He will rule over the house of Jacob forever and his reign will be without end."

But Mary could not see how all this would happen. And the angel said to her, "The Holy Spirit will come upon you and the power of the Most High will overshadow you; hence, the holy offspring to be born will be called Son of God. Know that Elizabeth your kinswoman has conceived a son in her old age; for nothing is impossible with God."

Mary was obedient. She knew that the angel was sent by God to tell her what God wanted. So she replied, "I am the servant of the Lord. Let it be done to me as you say." With that the angel left her.

As soon as Mary gave this answer, she became the Mother of God. The Second Person of the Blessed Trinity took to himself a body and soul like ours. He became Man and dwelt among us. This is called the mystery of the Incarnation. Mary is truly the Mother of God.

Discussion:

1. Who was Mary?
2. Who was Joseph?
3. What did the angel say to Mary?
4. Why did the angel say that Mary did not have to be afraid?
5. How did the angel say all this would happen?
6. What was Mary's answer to the angel?
7. What happened when Mary gave her answer?
8. Why is Mary the Mother of God?

C. PRACTICE

1. The devotion to our Blessed Mother which is especially dear to her and to her children is the rosary. The Hail Marys which we recite as we meditate on the mysteries of the life of Jesus and Mary are a means of expressing our love for them. We should make an effort to say the rosary each day. The Blessed Virgin herself requested that we say the rosary when she appeared to St. Bernadette at Lourdes, France and to the three children at Fatima, Portugal.

Jesus will come again to give us all to the Father

Part Eleven — DEATH, JUDGMENT, ETERNITY

CHAPTER

25 Final Reunion with God

158. **Why should we face death with courage and joy?**

(1) We have reason to live and to face death with courage and joy because the Lord's resurrection means that death has been conquered; (2) in the risen Christ we live, we die, and we shall live again; (3) we look ahead to a homecoming with God our loving Father.

(1) Death is the separation of body and soul from each other. We believe that death is the passage over the doorway of earthly life to the life beyond. Jesus gave death a new meaning, changing it into an event bringing salvation. He did this by becoming man and taking death on himself. In his death Jesus gave himself as a perfect sacrifice to the heavenly Father. As the second Adam by his glorious resurrection Jesus gained his final victory over the lord of death.

(2) The resurrection of Christ is the most important proof of our resurrection in the body. Through the merits of his Son God has set up his new order, according to which Jesus is to be the beginning of resurrection. St. Paul said, "Death came through a man; hence the resurrection of the dead comes through a man also. Just as in Adam all die, so in Christ all will come to life again" (1 Cor 15, 21-22).

(3) We should face death with courage and joy, looking ahead to a homecoming with God our loving Father. God made us for himself. Our highest happiness will be to be united with him forever in heaven, our true home.

159. What will happen when Christ returns with power?

When Christ returns with power as judge of the living and the dead he will hand over his people to the Father.

Jesus prophesied that he would return to earth one day in triumph to judge the living and the dead. His enemies will be forever conquered, and he will bring history to its appointed end.

160. Until the Lord's arrival in majesty, where will his disciples be?

Until the Lord's arrival in majesty, (1) some of his disciples are pilgrims on earth; (2) some have finished this life and are being purified in purgatory; (3) and others are in glory, beholding God himself.

(1) Some of our Lord's disciples are pilgrims on earth, journeying toward their heavenly homeland.

(2) At the very instant the soul leaves the body it is judged by Almighty God. This judgment is called the Particular Judgment. If we die without the least trace of sin upon our soul, the immediate sight of God in heaven will itself be our judgment.

Anyone who dies in the grace of God, but is not free from all sins and all punishment due for sins, cannot go to heaven at once. Those who still have to do penance for their sins go first to a place of cleansing which we call purgatory ("cleansing place").

(3) The beatific vision is an immediate vision of God. This person-to-person union with him is the happiness of heaven. The full flowering of supernatural life to which God in his mercy raised us is the future eternal life. This happiness for which man was created is eternal.

161. What will happen on the day of the last judgment?

On the day of the last judgment each person will reach his eternal destiny: all of us will be revealed before the judgment place of Christ, so that each one may receive what he deserves, according to what he has done on earth, good or bad.

All mankind will be judged at the end of the world by Jesus Christ, not only as God but also as man. Jesus himself taught us that he would be the judge of mankind.

God will reward everyone according to his works at the General Judgment, and will give eternal life to those who persevere in good works to the end. Our union with God will be so complete that we cannot now even faintly imagine the joy of it. We shall also know our loved ones in heaven.

162. What will happen to evildoers?

The evildoers shall rise to be damned in hell.

Having willingly cut itself off from God during life, the soul which has died without turning back to God has now no means by which to get in touch with God. It has lost God forever, having died without that bond of union with God which we call sanctifying grace. Hell is eternal separation from God.

163. **What will happen to those who have done right?**

Those who have done right shall rise to live a life eternally with God and will receive the good things that he has prepared for those who love him.

We believe that the just who have been made perfect through death and purgatory are now in heaven, though they have not yet risen in the body nor undergone the final judgment. We are called to glorify God in heaven in a perfect manner by love and self-surrender to him. God is the highest good that we not only shall know and love, but also live, in a mysterious sharing of his life.

164. **What do Christians look forward to during this life?**

During this earthly life, Christians look forward to their final reunion with God.

On his return, Jesus will raise from the dead the bodies of those who died in union with him. The Father will raise us up too because of Jesus, if we turn to Jesus in faith. Jesus promised that someday he would raise up all those who had been entrusted to him. By rising from the dead, they will share in his resurrection in the fullest way. When Jesus has subjected all things to himself, he will deliver his dominion to the Father.   *Teacher reference: Principal Elements, no. 108*

A. FILL IN THE BLANKS

1. (1) We have reason to live and to face death with ....
   because the Lord's resurrection means that ....; (2)
   in the risen Christ we ...., we ...., and we shall
   ....; (3) we look ahead to a .... (158)

2. When Christ returns with power as judge of the living and
   the dead he will .... (159)

3. Until the Lord's arrival in majesty, (1) some of his disciples
   are ....; (2) some have finished this life and are ....;
   (3) and others are .... (160)

4. On the day of the last judgment each person will reach ....
   ....; all of us wil be ...., so that each one
   may receive ...., according to what .... (161)

5. The evildoers shall rise to be .... (162)

6. Those who have done right shall rise to .... and will receive .... that he has prepared for .... (163)
7. During this earthly life, Christians look forward to .... (164)

B. BIBLE READING　　　　　　　　　Matthew 25, 31-46

The Last Judgment

Jesus told his disciples about his second coming. He said, "When the Son of Man comes in his glory, escorted by all the angels of heaven, he will sit upon his royal throne, and all the nations will be assembled before him. Then he will separate them into two groups, as a shepherd separates sheep from goats. The sheep he will place on his right hand, the goats on his left.

"The king will say to those on his right: 'Come, you have my Father's blessing! Inherit the kingdom prepared for you from the

"When the Son of Man comes in His glory, He will take His seat upon His royal throne."

creation of the world. For I was hungry and you gave me food, I was thirsty and you gave me drink. I was a stranger and you welcomed me, naked and you clothed me. I will ill and you comforted me, in prison and you came to visit me.'

"Then the just will ask him: 'Lord, when did we see you hungry and feed you or see you thirsty and give you drink? When did we welcome you away from home or clothe you in your nakedness? When did we visit you when you were ill or in prison?'

"The king will answer them: 'I assure you, as often as you did it for one of my least brothers, you did it for me.'

"Then he will say to those on his left: 'Out of my sight, you condemned, into that everlasting fire prepared for the devil and his angels! I was hungry and you gave me no food, I was thirsty and you gave me no drink. I was away from home and you gave me no welcome, naked and you gave me no clothing. I was ill and in prison and you did not come to comfort me.'

"Then they in turn will ask: 'Lord, when did we see you hungry or thirsty or away from home or naked or ill or in prison and not attend you in your needs?'

"He will answer them: 'I assure you, as often as you neglected to do it to one of these least ones, you neglected to do it to me.'

"These will go off to eternal punishment and the just to eternal life."

Discussion:

1. How did Jesus tell his disciples about his second coming?
2. What will the king say to those on his right?
3. What will the king answer when they ask when they did all these things?
4. What will the king say to those on his left?
5. What will the king answer when they ask when they saw him in need?
6. What will happen to those on the left?
7. What will happen to those on the right?
8. How does this parable tell of our final union with God?

C. PRACTICE

1. We should prepare ourselves to meet our Savior by trying to lead a holy life and by doing our part in spreading the kingdom of God. At his death each man gives an account of his life. Nothing decided at this final accounting will be changed in the last judgment.

2. All the means which will help us to live up to the ideals of Jesus Christ are here for us to use. The life-giving sacraments are here to give us holiness and strength. We should receive them often. Above all, the great source of grace and love, the Eucharist, is here for our daily use. Daily Mass will help us to be more deeply united to Christ and our neighbor. Help and encouragement will come to us from our union with God in prayer. People should be able to see in our lives the proof of our deeper union with God which comes from prayer. They should be able to see that we live by faith, that we are strengthened by hope, that we practice love of God and our neighbor in our daily life. We shall share in that final victory of Christ if we remain in union with him throughout our lifetime.

JESUS SPEAKS:

> "I am the way, and the truth, and the life; no one comes to the Father but through me. If you really knew me, you would know my Father also."   (Jn 14, 6, 7)

> "Be glad and rejoice, for your reward is great in heaven."
> (Mt 5, 12)

> "The Son of Man will come with his Father's glory accompanied by his angels. When he does, he will repay each man according to his conduct."   (Mt 16, 27)

APPENDICES

APPENDIX A

THE TEN COMMANDMENTS OF GOD

1. I, the Lord, am your God. You shall not have other gods besides me.
2. You shall not take the name of the Lord, your God, in vain.
3. Remember to keep holy the sabbath day.
4. Honor your father and your mother.
5. You shall not kill.
6. You shall not commit adultery.
7. You shall not steal.
8. You shall not bear false witness against your neighbor.
9. You shall not covet your neighbor's wife.
10. You shall not covet anything that belongs to your neighbor.

THE BEATITUDES

1. Blest are the poor in spirit: the reign of God is theirs.
2. Blest are the sorrowing: they shall be consoled.
3. Blest are the lowly: they shall inherit the land.
4. Blest are they who hunger and thirst for holiness: they shall have their fill.

5. Blest are they who show mercy: mercy shall be theirs.
6. Blest are the single-hearted: for they shall see God.
7. Blest are the peacemakers: they shall be called sons of God.
8. Blest are those persecuted for holiness' sake: the reign of God is theirs. (Mt 5, 3-10)

APPENDIX B

DUTIES OF CATHOLICS

1. To keep holy the day of the Lord's Resurrection: to worship God by participating in Mass every Sunday and Holy Day of Obligation:* to avoid those activities that would hinder renewal of soul and body, e.g., needless work and business activities, unnecessary shopping, etc.

2. To lead a sacramental life: to receive Holy Communion frequently and the Sacrament of Penance regularly— —minimally, to receive the Sacrament of Penance at least once a year (annual confession is obligatory only if serious sin is involved).*
—minimally, to receive Holy Communion at least once a year, between the First Sunday of Lent and Trinity Sunday.*

Note:

(Duties traditionally mentioned as Precepts of the Church are marked with an asterisk.)

The traditionally listed chief Precepts of the Church are the following six:
1. To assist at Mass on all Sundays and holy days of obligation.
2. To fast and abstain on the days appointed.
3. To confess our sins at least once a year.
4. To receive Holy Communion during the Easter time.
5. To contribute to the support of the Church.
6. To observe the laws of the Church concerning marriage.

3. To study Catholic teaching in preparation for the Sacrament of Confirmation, to be confirmed, and then to continue to study and advance the cause of Christ.

4. To observe the marriage laws of the Church:* to give religious training (by example and word) to one's children; to use parish schools and religious education programs.

5. To strengthen and support the Church:* one's own parish community and parish priests; the worldwide Church and the Holy Father.

6. To do penance, including abstaining from meat and fasting from food on the appointed days.*

7. To join in the missionary spirit and apostolate of the Church.

APPENDIX C

ESSENTIAL PRAYERS

Recommended by the
National Conference of Catholic Bishops

SIGN OF THE CROSS

In the name of the Father, and of the Son, and of the Holy Spirit. Amen.

THE LORD'S PRAYER

OUR Father, who art in heaven, hallowed be Thy name; Thy kingdom come; Thy will be done on earth as it is in heaven. Give us this day our daily bread; and forgive us our trespasses as we forgive those who trespass against us; and lead us not into temptation, but deliver us from evil. Amen.

HAIL MARY

HAIL Mary, full of grace! The Lord is with you; blessed are you among women, and blessed is the fruit of your womb, Jesus. Holy Mary, Mother of God, pray for us sinners, now and at the hour of our death. Amen.

DOXOLOGY

GLORY be to the Father, and to the Son, and to the Holy Spirit. As it was in the beginning, is now, and ever shall be, world without end. Amen.

THE APOSTLES' CREED

I BELIEVE in God the Father Almighty, Creator of heaven and earth; And in Jesus Christ, His only Son, our Lord; Who was conceived by the Holy Spirit, born of the Virgin Mary; Suffered under Pontius Pilate, was crucified, died, and was buried; He descended into hell; the third day He rose again from the dead; He ascended into heaven, sits at the right hand of God the Father Almighty; From thence He shall come to judge the living and the dead. I believe in the Holy Spirit; the Holy Catholic Church; the Communion of Saints; the forgiveness of sins; the resurrection of the body; and life everlasting. Amen.

ACT OF CONTRITION

O MY God, I am heartily sorry for having offended You, and I detest all my sins, because of Your just punishments, but most of all because they offend You, my God, who are all good and deserving of all my love. I firmly resolve, with the help of Your grace, to sin no more and to avoid the near occasions of sin.

ACT OF FAITH

O MY God, I firmly believe all the truths that the holy Catholic Church believes and teaches; I believe these truths, O Lord, because You, the infallible Truth, have revealed them to her; in this faith I am resolved to live and die. Amen.

ACT OF HOPE

O MY God, trusting in Your promises, and because You are faithful, powerful and merciful, I hope, through the merits of Jesus Christ, for the pardon of my sins, final perseverance, and the blessed glory of heaven. Amen.

ACT OF CHARITY

O MY God, because You are infinite Goodness and worthy of infinite love, I love You with my whole heart above all things, and for love of You, I love my fellowmen as myself. Amen.

HAIL, HOLY QUEEN

HAIL, holy Queen, Mother of mercy; hail our life, our sweetness, and our hope. To you do we cry, poor banished children of Eve. To you do we send up our sighs, mourning and weeping in this valley of tears. Turn then, most gracious Advocate, your eyes of mercy toward us. And after this our exile show unto us the blessed fruit of your womb, Jesus. O clement, O loving, O sweet Virgin Mary.

THE HOLY ROSARY

The Five Joyful Mysteries

(For Mondays, Thursdays; Sundays in Advent, and from Epiphany to Lent.)

1. The Annunciation—Luke 1, 28.
2. The Visitation—Luke 1, 42.
3. The Nativity—Luke 2, 7.
4. The Presentation—Luke 2, 28.
5. Finding in the Temple—Luke 2, 46.

3. THE NATIVITY
For the spirit of poverty.

1. THE ANNUNCIATION
For the love of humility.

4. THE PRESENTATION
For the virtue of obedience.

2. THE VISITATION
For charity toward my neighbor. **173**

5. FINDING IN THE TEMPLE
For the virtue of piety.

THE HOLY ROSARY
The Five
Sorrowful Mysteries

(For Tuesdays, Fridays, and every day during Lent.)

1. Agony in the Garden—Mark 14, 35.
2. Scourging at the Pillar—Mark 15, 15.
3. Crowning with Thorns—Mark 15, 17.
4. Carrying of the Cross—John 19, 17.
5. The Crucifixion—Luke 23, 33.

1. AGONY IN THE GARDEN
For true contrition.

2. SCOURGING AT THE PILLAR
For the virtue of purity.

4. CARRYING OF THE CROSS
For the virtue of patience.

3. CROWNING WITH THORNS
For moral courage.

5. THE CRUCIFIXION
For final perseverance.

THE HOLY ROSARY

The Five
Glorious Mysteries

*(For Wednesdays, Saturdays, and for
Sundays from Easter until Advent.)*

1. The Resurrection—Mark 16, 6.
2. The Ascension—Mark 16, 19.
3. Descent of the Holy Spirit—Acts 2, 4.
4. Assumption of the B.V.M.—Gen. 3, 15.
5. Crowning of the B.V.M.—Apoc. 12, 1.

3. DESCENT OF THE HOLY SPIRIT
For love of God.

1. THE RESURRECTION
For the virtue of faith.

4. ASSUMPTION OF THE B.V.M.
For devotion to Mary.

2. THE ASCENSION
For the virtue of hope.

5. CROWNING OF THE B.V.M.
For eternal happiness.

My ☧ words
Ω ✗ A
will not
pass away

Matthew 24:35